Twitters for a Lark

ALSO BY ROBERT SHEPPARD

POETRY
Returns
Daylight Robbery
The Flashlight Sonata
Transit Depots/Empty Diaries
      (with John Seed [text] and Patricia Farrell [images])
Empty Diaries
The Lores
The Anti-Orpheus: a notebook *
Tin Pan Arcadia
Hymns to the God in which My Typewriter Believes
Complete Twentieth Century Blues
Warrant Error *
Berlin Bursts *
The Given
A Translated Man *
Words Out of Time
Unfinish
History or Sleep — Selected Poems *

FICTION
The Only Life

EDITED
Floating Capital: New Poets from London (with Adrian Clarke)
News for the Ear: A Homage to Roy Fisher (with Peter Robinson)
The Salt Companion to Lee Harwood
The Door at Taldir: Selected Poems of Paul Evans *
Atlantic Drift: an anthology of poetry and poetics (with James Byrne)

CRITICISM
Far Language: Poetics and Linguistically Innovative Poetry 1978-1997
The Poetry of Saying: British Poetry and Its Discontents 1950-2000
Iain Sinclair
When Bad Times Made for Good Poetry *
The Meaning of Form in Contemporary Innovative Poetry

* TITLES FROM SHEARSMAN BOOKS

Twitters for a Lark

Poetry of the European Union of Imaginary Authors

conducted and co-created by

Robert Sheppard

in collaboration with

Jason Argleton, Joanne Ashcroft, Alan Baker, James Byrne,
Alys Conran, Kelvin Corcoran, Anamaría Crowe Serrano,
Patricia Farrell, Allen Fisher, S. J. Fowler, God's Rude Wireless,
Robert Hampson, Jeff Hilson, Tom Jenks, Frances Kruk,
Rupert Loydell, Steve McCaffery, Eiríkur Örn Norðdahl,
Sandeep Parmar, Simon Perril, Jèssica Pujol i Duran,
Zoë Skoulding, Damir Šodan, Philip Terry,
Scott Thurston and René Van Valckenborch

Shearsman Books

First published in the United Kingdom in 2017 by
Shearsman Books
50 Westons Hill Drive
Emersons Green
BRISTOL
BS16 7DF

Shearsman Books Ltd Registered Office
30–31 St. James Place, Mangotsfield, Bristol BS16 9JB
(this address not for correspondence)

www.shearsman.com

ISBN 978-1-84861-565-6

ACKNOWLEDGEMENTS
Some of these poems have appeared in *A Festschrift for Tony Frazer,*
Card Alpha, Pages, Poetry Wales, Shearsman, Stride, Tears in the Fence,
The Bogman's Cannon, The Wolf, and *X-Peri,* and in online videos
of various Camarade and Enemies collaborative readings.

Cover image: Ivaylo Dimitrov

Contents

Lost in Transit

The European Union of Imaginary Authors (EUOIA) was invented and presided over by the fictional bilingual Belgian poet René Van Valckenborch for his final project before his disappearance in 2010. Van Valckenborch, who made no attempt to conceal his constructedness, supposedly asked one poet from each of the EU states to write him a poem, in response to a quotation from Henri Lefebvre about space, which was then scheduled to be translated into Flemish (or occasionally French) via robot (online) translators and the resultant poem 'finalised' by Van Valckenborch before intended presentation on his EUOIA website.

Only five such 'translations' by these poets – who are themselves fictional – appear at the end of Van Valckenborch's collection *A Translated Man* (Shearsman, 2013), authored by Robert Sheppard, and they are represented in *Twitters for a Lark* by recent work. Sheppard, who from 2010-16 was President of the EUOIA, undertook to 'translate' the work of the remaining 23 EU poets as a collaborative enterprise, making use of the full list of poets drawn up, but not used, in the writing of *A Translated Man*. (Croatia joined in the intervening years, pushing the total number to 28.) Sheppard says, 'I would like to thank all of my collaborators, who have pooled their sovereignty, as it were, and constructed poems and people in so many different, educative and exhilarating, ways.' The range of collaborators is impressively wide, and this, in part, accounts for the uniqueness of each poetic voice.

Any anthology of pan-European work, even one limited by the borders of the EU, is going to be broad in its scope, and we hope this collection will both delight and demonstrate that. (The exception is the poetry of Frisland, which nevertheless aspires to membership, despite its dubious geographical status.) Humour can be found juxtaposed with horror, the political with the personal, the formalist with the liberated, in the arrangement dictated by Van Valckenborch's list. It is not my intention to draw attention to any particular works (such intervention would be invidious) but simply compare the effusive Oulipean procedures of Paul Coppens' versions of Van Valckenborch's quennets with the glum, misanthropic single sonnet of Hubert Zuba, or contrast the deft word choreographies of Cristòfol Subira's bilingual lyricism with Minna Käkkäinen's extensive and scientific Martian landscape poetry. Sophie Poppmeier's performative burlesque pieces seem as far as one can get from the conceptual austerity of Trine Kragelund's textual gatherings. Of course, such eclectic range is to be welcomed (there is no contemporary poetic paradigm, let alone an ever-closely unified Europoem), but it must be asked what commonality the collection displays, what is held in common. Obviously the spirit of the enigma that is (or was) Van Valckenborch hangs over the whole enterprise, and the conducting and co-creative presence of Robert Sheppard (himself one of the fictional European poets by the time the project concluded) is constantly guiding progress with his poetics of what he rather mysteriously calls 'multiform unfinish'. There is no need to take his jargon seriously, but neither may he be wished away from the work.

Many of the poems invoke 'history' as either muse or medusa, tool or rule, and it is an irony of history that brings these birdsong-like twitters to a final cadenza. In 2016, as the project reached its conclusion, the British EU Referendum in favour of what an ugly neologism called 'Brexit' – a 'Eurologism' might be a better term for it – led to a mirror exclusion in the ranks of the EUOIA, and Sheppard was expelled in a 'Shexit' coup (as it was aptly named by collaborator Scott Thurston), and replaced by the controversial fictional poet Hermes.

At the March 2017 EUOIA Conference in Vilinus, which I chaired, Hermes' fatal combination of narcissistic personality disorder, make-believe and financial corruption, led to the withdrawal of counterfeit EU funding and the sudden collapse, de-branding and disbanding of the organisation. Its famous five multi-coloured vowels were unscrewed from above the podium and, in my final discretionary act as chair, do-nated to the Rimbaud Museum in Charleville. They were lost in transit.

Jurgita Zujūtė

8

Martina Marković (1982-)   Croatia

Spomen

7

fleš za flešom prolamaju se zauvijek nove
vijesti: tinejdžeri navučeni na e-cigarete.
srbofobni stanodavci zapjenjenih zubi.
rezak bol pod naušnicom vraća me u stvarnost.
umakanje vesla u vodu. meki nabor
površine prostire se sve do čvrstog kopna.
kao da sunce korača kuhinjom boso:
ne pamtim da je baka ikad cmoknula
uvukavši obraze među žedne desni. sirotinjstvo
sjećanja. ne postoji nešto poput savršenog ubojstva.
za bivše ustaše što vezali bi me k'o snop
drva za ogrjev. pogledala sam ga onako
blesavo (spomen na tu hitru sekundu)
i više me nije bilo. na poleđini novčanice
povijest je zgužvana, pahuljasta.
beskrajno razmjenjiva. beskrajno pohabana.
oblak sitnih muha roji se nad natrulim marelicama.

(Back-translated into Croatian by Damir Šodan)

From *Memorials*

7

the broken news is breaking forever in flash
after flash: teenagers addicted to e-cigarettes.
serbophobic landlords with frothy teeth.
an earring pinches me back into reality.
a dip of an oar. the soft unrolling
of wavelet on steady shoreline. as if
sunlight passes through the kitchen barefoot
and grandmother never sucked on her
thirsted dentures. memory's beggary.
no such thing as perfect murder. for
the ex-Ustaše who would bundle me up
like firewood. I give him my daffy look
(memorial of this one rushing second)
and am gone. history creased
and flaky on the backsides of banknotes.
infinitely exchangeable. infinitely rubbed raw.
a cloud of fruit flies festers above the soft apricots.

26

crusts of soot, fatigued metal creaks along the sloped sides.
the town ticks over, adjusting itself with new technologies.
cyber-clean and shrink-wrapped the people
watch video-clips from the age of steam. a platform edge
dusted with snow. one red shoe points intently
down the tracks to chalice lights. dummy houses.
what more is this province but a colony
of cells? the buddleia browns like old wine.
we feel the dip of the lines. weight running
the length of the dead carriage-works.
of exile's militia winds no clean sweep. uncle Jovan
spat jail soap. fed a day of the whip, of grass-tufted mud.
we feel the sad eyes of a signal
peaked by shades. it blinks instructions. coded
to the marrow, we conjure warm rushes of steam.

riffs: history
after Damir Šodan

history as a speedy barmaid.
mute expressions of stone.
blondest wunderkind (1939).

in the horsetracks of a queen's
carriage. parping out its notes,
off-white, low contrabassoon.

history, the mouth that buries
my mouth, more lips than flesh,
the fart's eye over the arsehole.

*

the partisan accordionist clutches
his wheezing frame, pushed by
a rattle of buttons. old medals.

he's decorated with a flag but
the grey light unfeatures it. a skull
inside a skull inside a skull.

*

the old tamburica player cups
his frozen hands into a mouthpiece,
yells his definite proclamation. his final

declaration of independence. something
like reverence or guilt. grinning marionettes
tangled like idiots, cry out for recognition,

simply being there instead of wasting away
into darkness and indefinition. the spider
scuttles away from the ink stain.

*

thunder grumbles, the spider freezes.
cubes of jelly atop the butcher's cupboard.
time permeates even the permafrost

of the poem. a wedding plate,
a bride made of tatters. thick flap
of a hoarding torn in the gust.

*

history's illegitimate daughter
—the I does not belong to itself—
she bellied through the house

more like a cloud of cheesecloth
than a mother. wind's prune hook
scrubbing maples. writing is

tropism, fires from a woodlot.
who am I, mother at the sepulchre,
waving this european passport?

JAMES BYRNE AND ROBERT SHEPPARD

Sophie Poppmeier (1981-)   Austria

Two Burlesques

Book 3 Poem 7

With nothing but language, O dreamer,
I dive between these borrowed words;
I understand their beating in the skies
with its pure rough joy like birds.

I'm tolerant of your precious places:
by subtle fraud my future verse
will rise to keep my spangly wings
in mind, flickering on their course.

A messenger of cool dusk, this fan is
(it's the one way to you in every shot)
imprisoned by the flutter behind my taut behind,
the lusting gust that turns the plot,

but with whose brand some mirror shines
vertiginously racing;
it quivers, limpid in pursuit,
with monstrous kiss, unlacing by unlacing?

Invincible dust shakes most furiously from flesh
because no one is to be born after.
That gives me no pain, bursting out of stays
or relieved by my encore's naked laughter.

Therefore: this fan will bless you always,
so you may feel the fierce paradise;
the white flight shows with your idle hands free,
beneath your corsets' floreate ice.

After '*Madame Mallarmé's Fan Dance*'
music: Claude Debussy: 'Poisson d'or' from *Images* (Set Two)

Book 3 Poem 11

Deep sleep, then Queen Neveen's eyes
were serene. Her feet between the sheets
flexed, then peeped, gem-sleek. She
left the bed, entered her levee, flew.

Heels crept, eyes begged, her legs
kept the slender steps she'd left perfect.
She'd let the seventeen meek temple wenches teem.
They wept when she wept, cheered when

she cheered, were severe when she yelled.
The scenes were set: the senses tense,
the cee-dee screeched. (Salah Ragab's Jazz Band
ran bad ass art, that aslant sax and atabal!).

Neveen's cleft dress, her serpent belt, her steel fetters,
expressed her sex, her gender. The extreme
bend she effected: we peered, we felt. The secret
needled between her legs, cheeks swept the screen.

We were erect, we settled, entered the event,
exegetes feeling clever, then stressed, then spent.
Neveen's speechless eyes, her bejewelled chest;
yes, she jerked free, then fell: *they'll* tell the rest.

After *'Neveen's Levee'*
music: Salah Ragab and the Cairo Jazz Band: 'Neveen'

ROBERT SHEPPARD AND JASON ARGLETON

Book 4 Poem 3

after Lutz Seiler, for Tony Frazer his translator

Postwar snow on the Mozart Bridge today.
I thought of your poem. A dead dog bobbed,
whirling on the flood tide of the Danube,
its old song carrying me eastwards. Easter-

tide: we sport ears torn from domestic bunnies,
another postwar story surviving
for the Mayday parade of potemkin bonnets.
The past stares out from the empty bandstand.

But memory plays a marching anthem,
limping along with a dead childhood
on its leash. *The Russians are coming.*
With their sainted cosmonauts and their poison

umbrellas, isotopes hidden in toy hippos. Under
the desks, the class of '81 hid, reading pre-war graffiti
and picking at scabby knots of chewing gum. A
bottle of strontium milk and only 6 seconds to wolf it.

No such luck: we climbed out again, stretching
into freedom that was fortified at its fraying edges,
some line drawn across the local mountains
from the songs that gathered around the skirts of the statues.

If you had not existed you would still have made me up!
And today, an April river-wind would still rip from the East.
A swan ruffles its feathers, buries its beak in blue, points
to where my poems sink like a sack of drowning puppies.

ROBERT SHEPPARD

Paul Coppens (1980-) Belgium

Four Quennets for Filip Dujardin
after René Van Valckenborch

risen ceiling   descending beards   riven tile
                      remedial enclosures

stained floorboards   garnished scallops   milky horizon
                      indistinguishable quadrilaterals

ghosted ringbinders   flesh cabinets   blooded giros
                      encrusted teacups

Hosts of the dead
boss the
vacuous shivers
without salt-filled snowballs
0.0002
buskers and uncountable
ancient micro-seconds

tarnished horizon   realisable drafts   transparent proposals
                      stuffed rafts

entombed spatula	synthetic lathering-device	insalubrious lather
	bouncing carvers	
fictitious chumps	ulcerated relish	Tupelo honey
	Sarson's bluebottle	
lamentable dependency	toxic medicaments	entombed counterfoils
	vitriform daggers	

But the freezer hisses
like a drug-crazed chef
Atop a what-not whatsits
and their girls Friday ponder
the powder of dilapidation and
break five Hoover bags
half a dozen poop-scoops

| saurian existence | esoteric suckers | silverware ladles |
| | peroxide pickles | |

given shoe-shredder   continuous carbon   clear mist
smutty arse-flannel

bored whisper   fleshly florescence   boring closure
belladonna cleavage

sea urchin   lymphatic catacomb   short-lived maturity
cataract mist

Cushions unlike sea portals
spread around singular reality
A clear view of
a carpet illuminates the nights
miniature chests of drawers
excluding a peep from somewhere sun-
hats that have never dried out

short-lived integrality   Germanic trouser-press   antelucan winter
cracked monocle

spireless spires   artless murals   stirring cabbage-patch
crystalline salt

same-old same-old   graffitied walls   sapphire boulevard
tyre-marked fur

tellurian work-ethic   boot mud   fingerprinting work-glove
unmarked gravel

Archive of insomniacs
deposited in the skip
with senescence
junked LPs
re-released on a flat plane
dropped on crushed fingers
with a 0.3 second noise-thrash
Canoes slide into the canal

rooted immovables   sunk can   reclaimed sandbank
carved pain

PHILIP TERRY AND ROBERT SHEPPARD

Ivaylo Dimitrov (1979-)   Bulgaria

Behind into Beyond

left right   Botev the horse & the back end of the
                                    trabant
                                           the socialist centaur
trot split
kiss my beginning   *cognitive volition*
bend me   green
                 red
                                    red wine heavy on the oak table
plant me
flowers on
my sky   blue   fomented breeze
on which I roll

the world in
three
small balls

what we know is what we

                                    masked by our own immunity
slice through the grills

                                         forced across our eyes

pink

         green

                                held up by wires
props steadied by strings

LOOK   see

                            roped in tight
smoothed out

along the road   motion is effortless

behind the trees   bent into strange alphabets

23

green-pink

my scuffed trainers under your face

turn fork

touch me

morning in the circle cut into it

back into my middle
behind into beyond

your gaze judges absurdity
singly

the mirror of my mother

land leap   your children's mobile above their plastic dinosaurs my father's smile

the clock that tells
three shining discs

left let's kiss
running right hover hop

floating home
yellow flower

photograph it's a cheap wedding long ago

leading to communal apartment blocks

remember the pattern on the carpet it will
guide you through the metal doors into death it's a map showing everything you
have faithfully forgotten

PATRICIA FARRELL AND ROBERT SHEPPARD

Gurkan Arnavut (1978-)

Cyprus

While Egrets Rise

While egrets rise under my eyelids
and the clock needles its way
into morning, it's as if weather
is all I've ever lived. When history
is a flip of last year's calendar
doing service again as a ladder
up this year's spine I cringe
before diurnal crests unctuous foam.
While every hour is water incessantly
returning every spring a loosening of
pins that hold the joints in place where
the tide turns on every bristle of my
wings tense against lover or prey
neck twisted like toilet plumbing the blaze
of scissored beak and beaded eye glides
to lock my claws around the bough for waiting.
Inland the dry ground turns in on itself
to warbler and wheatear the hoopoe's
spread wing. In time every song finds
its own way through the cracked air
to the cracked ear, even the hoopoe's,
triplets of dull barbs tracking on a green
string across a screen, 23 seconds
of filtered white noise behind which
wings rustle with the soft rush of
disappearing cash. Change is no change
at all shriek the birds disappearing into
money into the sky's indivisible walls.

Not Just the Suitors

Not just the Suitors. Their lovers too the bad maids
strung up along a cable {epic simile} like birds caught
in a net in a thicket till their legs stopped wombs
dropped. Like civilisation my compatriot Aphrodite
born from a cut. We're still on the line where the page
thickens towards forgetting / a starfish city split
by spilt foam washes at the edges. When carrying
this graft of atrocity and other aphrodisiacs
we're aphotic with despair aphonous with grief
a writhing tongue lashing ourselves to the mast
listening to keel's creak / wheel's squeak / sail's frap
and swooning in the void where the voices should be.
Pop songs from minarets: the channel switches mid-
current in saturated waves {braced notes} the call
to prayer never so loud as in its tuning out. Whose
love comes through the cables / in what frequencies
on the wave spectrum jostling for decibel-music / with
what frequency do trim voices bleed into prime time?
Do they scissor 'the price of the Euro decision for the
{celestial static} haircut of Greek debt'? No doubt
the other walks beside me and the other's other
slices through the shadows / each step cutting through
the space between heartbeats / in constant deficit {love
owed}. No ownership is not barbaric / no love not debt /
no cable of yellow electric bulbs stretched across the carnival
not darkened by smoke haze. Dimmed in hermaphroditic
indifference desire dissolved in equity the other becomes
the same in toxic exchanges of war graves {peace claims}.
From hand to hand my trembling right becomes tangential
to the act. Who am I if not this beginning on a table where
different worlds come into view / do-it-yourself death mask
beyond the glass of tea / not in the room but part of it.
Half of me slips from the stool. The poem shatters
and its worlds flatten on the fifth wall of space / time
demands she drops a headscarf leaving the table / its moment
won't return though she will to find it neatly folded
{double surface}. In the soft threads of another life

we cover and uncover the details that will never hold
together / each one unravelling its own past. Yes / this
means you. Or the cat wandering into no-man's land
sinewy with insinuation her soft pads assimilating
human ground. Hot towel on your face at the barbers / you
hear the sharpening of cut blades and hope your muffled
defence 'I am not Stavros Monopolous' will save you.

ZOË SKOULDING AND ROBERT SHEPPARD

Jitka Průchová (1978-)   Czech Republic

Ten Full Throated Odes

after the collages of Jindřich Štyrský

'iconoclasm – with scissors' (JŠ)

1 *Genesis*

Amid bubbling
Magma rings
On cooling
Meniscus rising through a hole
Of its own
Engendering a phallus sniffs
The air stiff and
Veiny the god of creation
Feels the first breeze
Brushing its glans

2 *Scopophilia*

Eyes set deep in
Jellabas fanged
Fish snap
Where she pulls her
Flesh apart to stretch
The mollusc on her
Labia safe in its frame
The image of itself
Closed
To every impression
But the eyes'

3 *Bohemian Shores*

The seashore seethes
And roars where the twins
Bathe heads lost in
Crashing sea-foam
Beached goodie-two-shoes
Planted well apart love-sick
Whales thighs
Open to the esplanade
Where promenaders pause
To absorb the salty breeze

4 *Tiny Alabaster Hand*

Inside the inside
Boxes within the master
Geometry of the room flesh
Within flesh within
The human pyramid fucks
Inside itself moulded
In passion's grip
Holding whole to desire's
Strictest measure

5 *Picture Postcard City Gallery Prague*

A wall of eyes in
Vitreous night melting
Retinal screen
Forces lovers to
Enflesh each other
Abrades their single skin
In one collective
Bl-
Ink

6 *The Fall*

She floats jewel-encrusted
Pumps awry
A dildo pushing at
Pulsing ingress too late
For she's falling already ecstasy
Impressed in cloud
On her melting eyes a hooked
Leg rises but falls
The other is pinched by
A diving dove lips
Pinned to a parachute
Dry as they drop –
Not telling –
Crinkled pucker –
Plunging

7 *The Man Fed On Ice Hots Up*

The soprano sings through
Electric hair spreads
Arms wide till she
Touches the hand
Of the naked tenor who
Spins like a cosmonaut
In a solar storm the aria
Flows across the coupling below
Buttocks tense
Masculine but
Shyly anonymous as a vagina
Clears itself
For full-throated odes

8 *Pornophilia*

A light-bulb screwed
Into bursting pods
Blossoms hangs limp in
Interstellar vacuum
Over the threesome busy
Flicking and sucking
Heads bowed to the
Script one finger
Sparks a node of flesh
Shoots impulse as sharp
As pain across the
Pleasure-dome a crouched
Mouth
Accepts
The star-burst

9 *Emilie Comes to Him in a Dream*

She shields her face
From the skull
With her fan lush
Gloves unfurling it
One breast
Visible her thigh-
Length stockings dust
The skeleton
Laid out with her as
If paired for love
A shoulder bone axe
Lies dislocated
A tattered boot sclerotic
At a knee swelling
In the hollow between hip joints
A penis mushrooms the
Only impulse
Left in the marrow
Is procreative death

Swimming beyond the
Planets among
The stars the Olympian
Stirs
Crackles of light they
Tingle
Her clitoris the naked woman
Curls around it
Spinning
In vacancy thighs
Clamping
But it peeps
Its blind eye turning
To the last touch
Of creation and comes

ROBERT SHEPPARD

Trine Kragelund (1979-)   Denmark

Wax Poetics

How do I create annotations? There's nothing new under the sun. You would have no power over me if it were not given to you from above. No! by Thomas Hood. No sun – no moon! No morn – no dinner! No dawn—no other edits outside this topic! They are encouraging you not to edit a particular page or part of a page. Fidelity no longer has initial charges on any of the funds available on our fund supermarket. It wasn't Hitler's intention to force a war with Denmark or to take over its polyglot discourse which was amusingly interrupted by a cuckoo clock. There are two groups of nouns that have no singular form. *Nouns* is our first LP as Weirdo Rippers. Registers that may be labelled 'modern Copenhagen street speech' are also the varieties that have spread most rapidly in the past century. The design is that no flesh should glory in his presence, no flesh be justified in his sight. You saw no form on the day that the Lord spoke to you. No more silo mentality in an ivory tower. This conference is sponsored by the Council for Independent No Things. Hi, my name's Gyda. I'm a Thinker for News 101. Two psychologists lament their profession's involvement in torture and abuse at Guantánamo. After apologizing for his comments comparing increased taxation on the rich to the Nazi pogrom of Kristallnacht, he took a Vow of Silence. No More Symptomology: I'm back to reality after a nice weekend away at my father-in-law's beach house. The failure of homologous chromosomes or sister chromatids to separate subsequent to metaphase in meiosis or mitosis so that one daughter cell has yucky workspaces (one was a tiny office with no windows, the other a messy room which hardly had baby steps). No rogue plumbers are fit for this job. A British woman's belly button explodes on a plane, but Denmark bans halal slaughter. No; only a small percentage of mutations cause genetic disorders, like these three letters: *oem, ems, nos, nom, oms, nms, nes, noe, oes.* The new sedimentologically based curve shows no transgressive deposits are partitioned landwards, in the west. Five letters: *norms, poems, nones, noses, notes, nodes.* Angels have no philosophy but love. Gnomes? No Passion: all Technique. All anger: no technique. Empathy MeetUps near Roskilde. Elves? Fools find no pleasure in understanding but delight in airing their own opinions, take no pleasure in the strength of a horse or in human might. No Life King: all death anchor. Pixies? A Somali who is no good for anything – that is simply not acceptable. A poet uses punctuation not so much for grammatical correctness but rather for enjambment mud. Mud is mud or the thinking of a poem is the poem. Crucifixion is not no fiction. So-called chosen frozen. Just wondering if anyone has ever been to a rave without taking anything and remaining totally sober. I am social. I am inspired. Which country are you in? No? Copenhagen gender quotas make it easier to be hired as a woman professor. Scientists say that in one particular test *goats* are quicker on the uptake than *chimps*. Sorry, I thought you said, 'No *coats* allowed.' I am no poet. I do not love words for the sake of words. I love words for what they can accomplish. Similarly, I am no arithmetician. Figures speak only of love's serenity. Black Danish warships like a storm-cloud lay, as Miss Kay serves her home cookin' from a food truck, and the Duckmen go on strike. World leaders fought the great Copenhagen Fudge. Many ships have been hijacked, crew members attacked. Measurements of noise from mainly Danish-produced wind turbines are relatively stable. You know what chickens mice are. What does 'love keeps no record of wrongs' mean in terms of how I show love to others? A Danish Scientist breaks the 9/11 culture of silence: our law prohibits the security services from being involved in assassinations. There are no quantum jumps, nor are there particles! The number of maximum entropy applications in our field has grown. This map shows us the places where no one—really, no one—lives.

Robert Sheppard

Mussolini Among the Muses

I puff out a simple blues on my pipes
in the Lydian mode. My legs sport eyes
like bees, I know I am me despite the hive
mind. I smoke myself out of torpor,
exercise the poet's blink in the dark. I sail
like a radio wave, an anti-angel blocking the sun
as I track my echoing speck across the land.

My flight plan is erratic, I hover to inquire
into what I see, what catches my attention
as I fly through the world. Radar and sonar
cannot confine my senses to the fivefold ratio.
My wings fan. I dive invisible to human eye;
my message drips like honey as I drop.
I wax eloquent, am like no other you know,

soar in the shape of paradise, harmonizing
as mathematicians did of yore. Your
equation is a riddle to be solved, in the CCTV
of my high eye, the pixellations of a grey alley
below, computing the lo-res transgressions
much as I sin against myself. The fever dream
of self sweats out my soul, I am all yours,

all on edge, nasty with innuendo, as I salute
the classical statues rimming the stadium I circle:
a Mussolini among the Muses, I sing, frothy with frills,
frantic to fly as music to the stars. I contort myself
into poetic shapes, stretch as I scatter the spores of relief,
swooping hawkish to my birdwoman's nest, an olive branch
for the kitchen dropping from my beakish snout.

Poles Apart

There is something alive under the bed
and I press my ear to the pillow to keep
it out. It is not inspiration or love, it
might be a mud-faced creature, its snub-nose
sniffing me, rodent cognition in its whiskers.
A pumping thought excites my body –
perhaps it is desire personified, perhaps
it is the past come to haunt me? I know
only that past desire peeps through a curtain
and, seen from behind, it leans across a table,
a saucy painting of a courtesan espied by a
policeman who plays with his truncheon
and longs to use his power to arrest.
Handcuffs dangle in my mind as something
jangles under the bed. The long arm of some law
could curl around me to administer its
non-consensual anti-sensualist anarchic
hold. Consider the value of self, the way
we move through the world, how we hold
and nurture the white bear that peers through
our portholes, pawing at our circles of light.
There's nothing he can claw back, nothing
more likely to polarise us. I am sure
there is something alive under the bed,
and I am sure it is me.

RUPERT LOYDELL AND ROBERT SHEPPARD

Minna Kärkkäinen (1974-) Finland

Small Choruses on Mars

My body
is a series
of metaphors flows
and floods battered
ornaments
of up and
down in and out left
and right
the champion bedroom
of a fat dictator before breakfast

Sat wondering where I was in
myself what was
the brine taste in my mouth why
did the horizon lift and drop
in my head thought
what's inside my rib cage
characteristics beyond generic
determination beyond material
content and neck pulse on this
plane pulls back my impulsion

organ alone stops thought
looking down where one's feet
rolled out onto the surface or not
the camera is not just an eye
relinquishing the smallest exception
to the sandy arm and leg
and the stretched mind that's
the smallest weathered stone
Only the eye roams here
thinking 'bone' but believing data

Overwhelmed webbed light and
are they dust trails
so many they form go same
window blinds so much
so my cough improves in continuity
sucking more pumped gas
infiltrated with marsh air
or it is imagined substrate
cellular exactness
counted in patterned form

Dawn and dusk or otherwise slim
which nestles along
its bed of shade as if a filter
had been placed across the sky
by a baggy mother
hungry recognitions
like the light on Mars now
too many hours spent with her
skull split the sun a rumour
like a breakfast egg

Sat in a warm suit wonder
of my love melts
in the ice of its flame
softening the surface
trail of prints and embossings
the colophon of a boot heel
crushing cold into cold
crunch as I imagine it
from this stiff wear
bu bubbled in wraps

To obstruct us nothing
those three occasions he'd witnessed
eclipses to paw the floor in

the dark together with the obligation
to move out in the yard with his canvas and pinhole
to flex an eye muscle toward the curved horizon
projecting the slice of smile
from the sun's face fixed
to my image too sharp to be sewn
to which this crash-rubbish stretched out

in my self own skin
in my suit as a contrast
what you want me to do
got this language gap
relation to what what to
in the cosmos surrounded
almost but not of this world
burnt hands from
some of this burnt tongue
like I was over there

also like a kind of open room
grows large as the eye
sees in a like for like
beyond touch
instead of contained
in the envelope of surface
ontologically neutral void
anticipates isotropic awe
integrates measure
with perception

Speculation begins cosmology
until the helicopter ambulance
ships her broken bones
as rhetoric 'terrain' is an assumption
reduced to geology
everything is metaphorical in in

miniature. Did I remember
a button dropped under a dresser
navigating between the snags
and abrasions

Being here roots
tap a row of tracks
destructed into a
distant sequence
towards and away from
my diary and invented
future food supply
unsettled in the dust
here resettled as it
moves or as this winds

a squash of blood craters
pocks the rough sandy
planet's winter sunlight
see-sawing between life and death
between the larger obstacles
it could be a range of hills
or mountains holding a treatise
by Kant up to its poor eyes
or a hillock or two or the ulcerated mouth
that dribbles treacle into my lap

Can't make out
when this could be
counting the clock-hand
impression that a concept
like time can calibrated without
realising its context in those
glimmers of light exception
to the roar of the sun
disturbs what can be
seen broken in shift rhythms

like a shadowy depression
of a pebbledash wall of
public housing in Espoo
a oneway ticket to erosion
ig igneous concentration
where I've landed a gift a
threat a surprise his light would dim
onto his serge like a star
or a triangle filled with birds
falling silent in a beer can glint

I feel rested the result from
affection now mine loosened
from myself my weight
in the gravitas on this aridity
frightened by it absorbed
in its circumstance its heaviness
and heat as if belongs to
where we are in having it
thought of as human
in a given desert

Hunched as we are
smooth or jagged rocks
empurpled
thinking in close-up
bruise-light blue washes
of force across them
going in closer to see less and less
to reveal more
striations across the whole
until we're looking at a rumour hill

Would like to go for a walk
but that's not easy
maybe make fast-food breakfast

dust of egg with plastic bacon
maybe a rubber sandwich
using hardened paper utensils
and a grin or grimace occupy
inner sphere what to do
to get out of it into what
would that be what gasp

What on the pitted screen of
micro-craters, dark trenches? Like
the footprints of a flat-footed sure-footed
[   ]
that stands, sinking in sand,
bellowing to the sky,
a sky that is not The Sky
but space
singing the wind
blows high and space that isn't

In apprehension openness
to which things matter encourages
bleakness up against prospection
you see the horizon wobble
and the flavour of breakfast
drops into a tureen of explosions
squeezed through a tube
enhanced by planetary impacts
beneath the surface beyond
my comfort zone

ALLEN FISHER AND ROBERT SHEPPARD

Domiciled at Intervals

les langues orientales
du monde arabe
       I prefer
her silence curled up
impenetrable
little white feet
on a silk carpet
the divan—hooks lighting
      a face
gifted by the serial despair
of imperial afflictions
her deaf camisole
little white feet
      driving me senseless

white   space a girl

in a dufflecoat and shiny DMs
txts   neck bent crouched
over the miniscule screen in her palm

her digit-patterns bounce
around the globe   back again

don't stop until they hit a pocket

where jigsaw eyes leave imprints
in soft clay
erect poles amid
innocent trees   cracked marble
(home)

the icon   the totem   the toy
glows

won't answer

far off *tutoiment*   the jist she is
blank monument in catafalque   skin
getting away

white I   dream of
papered names
the sleepless rim of *maison*
         her cold strobe
         a nucleus

lamps domiciled   at intervals
was once
a road breathing

she sucks this tongue
         dry she shudders
bubbles of excitement bounce
down the road
                  of excess
                  moist-lipped
                  she repels
resistant to his gaze
kohl
eyelashes unleashing resistance –

the body of an arab rocks at high tide
the foot of the white cliff

eyes bloated bright
         with white

I look   fail to look
after all   she is not blank

                    a painted kimono
purple egrets   unknowable script
        flows full from her waist

              into this scene
              I pour

the waters off Lesbos
divine the hour
as stateless

              my body ashore in the foam
down the Boulevard du Magenta

the block
                    whipped harder
                    than a man's
intimate knees
              drops as a tangle
                                        cloying
yearning on the tarmac
                    the vast arches
of *la gare* push up daylight
glimmers through the curving network
of iron welcomes
                              non-people
play at waiting by high-backed benches
dawdling on capacious stairs   beneath clocks

mottled as sentences   stare from rocks
monuments countenance me also   where I

moored at dusk   with Laval's *relève*   *les deportées*
Vichy underlined as calculable flaw

hamartia   riven moral arrow
fraternité

Atropos

I speak her name   and still
        her white fingers on the console
                are processing—

five painted blades fastened to the state

digitally enhanced image faces you
down on Facebook
        girls
dancing
                across a swastika
a solitary egg rests
        in the morning's fireplace
her books turned
titles to the wall   a performed
                silence to Morta

dignatories arrive at the gym
        where she cleans
like neon circling a bust of Napoleon

banlieues radiate   a chaos *asiatique*
imbricate serpent logic   enfattened
singed meat   turning on a spit

she returns home
little feet   pale roots
terroir   that is hers

        charnel
        phosphate
        explodes

obscene immeasure of   what means
I have   walked
                three continents
for

this silent evening   lit up
     by voices   elsewhere
change:

'sensitive urban zones'
the serpent
        announces 'could burn again'
        she's
        hugging the serpent tree for balance

gripping the apple earth
           with little swollen feet

the pasty body of bloodless myth
corpses

           the corsair ravishes *qui?* –
a silent film in a palace of light
bleaches
           the blisters on her toes

SANDEEP PARMAR AND ROBERT SHEPPARD

Karla Schäfer (1972-)   Germany

Frances Kruk and Robert Sheppard

Eua Ionnou (1971-) Greece

Allophones 1

Even my name announces a history of human capacity
a dance upon the mouth music scales meaning nothing,
or the name of he who named me, a lost sheep seeking a shepherd.

I also know, at some point in the palsied future,
a damn believer will champion this is as the great motif;
thus dead metaphors choke us all – why misread the dumb beast?

However, this aside, you must listen to my morning broadcast
for I have recharged the arcane batteries of Radio Mystras
and reconstructed on the brimming air the marvels of Byzantium.

Lesson 1: you must not become a hired mouth or pundit,
if so you will assume the loathed shape of the vile opposition
and be a singing bird in a cage eating its own droppings.

Lesson 2: you must remember only archaeology holds final truth
and that it is denied us, mere stones, abandoned towns, archaic gas
but that the meaning of an unread inscription can change everything.

Good: the valves are humming and the meters flicker,
the dust burns, I tap tap the microphone – you can hear me,
you can hear these words remade on pulses of morning air.

Allophones 2

As surprising as the small pool of cool water
found high in the mountains, that bright ellipse
keeping a cold eye on the arching blue,

So with this marble slab below the cathedral dome,
fit place to make a last emperor stand and spin;
a trapdoor into which everything will come to fall.

From the softening of resistant terms flows decay
but if history is an account of the drift of phonic change
it can be read backwards to the well of meaning.

Though celebrants are replaced by pale readers
replaced by an audience of gibbering half-wits
and the paraphernalia of cultivated anti-thought.

Constantinople, Mystras and Sparta's ruin
atomised into the reconstruction of dead sound,
the dust of which clouds the air above the plain.

Lesson 3: you must trust the people, their erudition
from unlikely sources, from the stream of first meaning
into the mouths of all the people under the ringing sky.

Allophones 3

Listen to my call sign: rolling in the surge and surf
of the 41 metre band, phasing and re-phrasing
the stutter I transmit over and over: this is Radio Free State,

Keeping the channel open like a scooping dredger,
clattering buckets of filth. The evening broadcast
stands on the shore throwing pebbles at distant islands,

Enveloped in more myth than my poor voice can pretend.
Yet as the hour approaches and the call sign fades
then I must face up stiffly to the new headlines,

Wait for the green light and grimace my way through.
The edges of Europe have again been flecked with the pain
of those who wish to bathe in the opulence of our bailout.

My teeth click an undersong in ancient Morse, and it's done,
And you hear bitterness as the dusk fattens and falls.
Lesson 4: you must send me a QSL request now now now.

Rate your reception 1-5. Perhaps it will never matter what I say.
Perhaps you will one day not need to listen. Perhaps
your own breath will weave an amulet of illegible truth.

Allophones 4

Lesson 5: you must chant uncaged birdsong, stutter
homophonic harmonies and intone glyphic Byzantine hymns.
Full of meaning, you'll finally understand nothing,

Like Radio Tirana jamming the year of my birth
with Maoist jetsam, or the grandchildren of the last emperor
wondering what all the echoing frescoes might mean.

The Northern Despots take what they will from this disaster:
gluts of guestworkers for their ageing cities, crusted with snow,
or a few token cripples for charitable show from the war-zone.

The victories of socialist leaders who don't wear ties,
Persian chic in our ancient portals, shouldn't deceive us.
Just before the Shipping Forecast I'll slip in a plug for them –

It'll do them no good, given who writes the news.
It will sail unnoticed, out to sea, archaic goods of liberty
and equality, a World Tour dressed down as anti-Odyssey.

Listen: Mystras is calling. Aerials high above the Palace thrum.
Lesson 6: I must unscript my bulletin and sing from the grove where
my heart lies buried between the Ottoman and King Otto.

KELVIN CORCORAN AND ROBERT SHEPPARD

Ratsky József (1970-)   Hungary

opus 105

I ratsky jósef on the avenue
du chant d'oiseau there I wept
when I remembered záhony

1,000 km from its rusting loco-
motives beached on their stunted rails
funnels boilers & frozen pistons

like the modified organs of the
church of our lady of the end
of the world ma belle bruxelles

the fluted pipes rise into the air
& my breath rises with them as
I sink to my knees before the keys

it's dóra antal's birthday she doesn't
worry about the corno inglese she
doesn't worry about the contrafagotto

does worry about the water music
the birthday cake its chocolate bite the
chorine zurna circular submarine breathing

up periscope down with magyar posta &
the interurban messages of the hungarian
kings for 25 euros I will show you my ears

for 15 euros I will palm my old photos of
buda manholes the word *elektromos*
curving as the music swells from below

opus 119

press one key hear the note plangent
as though distant over the silver EU
complex a thin line un-swollen un-
stopped fading amidst 12 gold stars

and the closed down institute of regular
canons oh to be in Gödöllő now that winter's
here incomplete and painted like a world
peace gong or un-English onion dome

the player in the cap is known for his
fancy flick-knife work the other is
fond of dungeons and swells in echoic
chill a dank walled timbre falling

and rising in the electric measuring
factory up and down the manuals
with a stopped diapason the cap is
adjustable the other is compound

at the end of one thing as it turns into no
thing scored across the vista rendered faces
loom this organ regulates the pupil who
learns human flared only on the blink

no on the brink of something round
and rich and almost free his racket bright
and silvery had a pear shaped head and
echoey cor de nuit-like brazen clang

do not confuse my nachthorn with their
nachthoorn and its stocks and shares do
not donate your organs at the scene of
road-kill never say pull out the stops to

gerard of csanad his long long life has
blocked the pipes of my hungarian guy –

being alive – refusing the quo – pierced by
a lance – 12 gold bars carried us through

JEFF HILSON AND ROBERT SHEPPARD

Sean Eogan (1969-)   Ireland

Antlered He Goes (AE IOU)

ALL the Spirits mounting Guinness
breath-hearty sing my rhyme's assumption
ONLY playing hide and seek on out we go
past BREXIT as the Courts pass time

Fair Lennon, when my fleets
go through your spangled wordland
'Tis your Mayor Cloudy's feet I feel
on Dewy flecks AND on fire

in the moonshine his smile growls
the central part of pearly-dusty rays
BUT Meetings slide and speak at Samhain
some frolicking February boy AND girl

when I step Into the Word
some showers' Mysterious radiance
from the jewel treachery verbs a sleeping heart
THROUGH the veils of darkened houris

for the twilight gleams on the drinking school
meeting by The Sanctuary well-wrought
/Head BUTTS the Beamish/Knock need the Murphy's/
whispers well in this widdershins heat-haunt

some ships continue to sail in beauty
meeting saponaceous flying TRAILS
some Sun there efforts you only
for the Song-Self I lose you in

The Lake of Innesfree

A cold kiss + a handshake
concocts a weird front for reticence.
Time to Gestapo
getapotato clock
swift as the gulliver travels then on it is
to Brendan's minnow pond

to drain it dry.

Wind in the willows, no?
the zound you hear (do you heer it)
is your good self passing gas as you
pull down the cartage he billet & kood
turn the should have beans into has beens

the chaos will be handled by Messrs
Clay and Wattle, they
who worked hard to free
Innis from Guiness
by a dozend dozes of honey to go

content he was on the buzz honey bee-lines
in a swigswam
content in the drips of the drops
from the cirrus and syrup
at open eye time
to sing a maiden over till
the witching hour and the day again
croak croke against eventide
as in it a linnet.

Sure his get-up-and-go has got-up-and-gone
and his hears are full of it sun to moon
('tis the Guinness again)
thrown out on the strait and the peevment
where he's hearing the core of it

TAIF XUL

ni tceferp esrever natal

STEVE MacCAFFREY AND ROBERT SHEPPARD

Lucia Ciancaglini (1968-2010)   Italy

From &

(poem five)

& noise is not the message the brushing of rain
       the conditions of utterance are the real conditions
& the world shines filled with impenetrable zeroes

& there's one verdict of a sort the drop to vernacularity
       scissor-jawed protractions at every point a sign
& all my worldly works and days I'll spill upon my son

& there is no translation at work just scanning
       infinite space opens enclosed at tight fingertips
& exile leads to further exile with the technocrats' paddles

& I disappear into utility & biography
       feigning space in extension across unpitched time
& rattling keys like the janitor of the latest retail outlet to close

& I rest all morning nestling my lava java
       an empty sleeve salutes the cosh of exclamation
& cogs within cognition spit forth these forms

& an ampersand ghosted on the wall over from the coffee shop
       is a hollow in a headlock with nothing to say to us
& there's too much for the mind to do each second

& my son crayons the zero round & round & round &
       knuckling gloves on my lip gloss tease my melting eyes
& patterned interferences wipe the bootprint off my smile

& framed by sculpted hair I wait for the sky to drop
       to flood my bleached floss with grey light
& a lash of uncoiling ampersand cracks in the slanted hail

& an orthography of near-identical letters shakes amid
       iron bolts & marble kerbing frenzied docksides
& backstreet barbers amid ribbons & streamers

& I realise now that I don't exist like Cinderella or
       Catarella caught in a revolving door
& these pumice stones on my tongue weigh less than they ought

& shift the categories off-message across my bared back
       adverts punctuated by pimples & boils
& my body has no words repairing below compromised skin

& trees frenzied by gales hurl nuts & torn twigs
       moist with affront
& my flinch is like touch itself turned inside out for cleansing

& an orgasm of lightning printed on un-hydrated flesh
       moulds me into a bony maquette of electric desire
& my lips that stick learn to smile at appropriate calibrations

& the hole is a device to grip two or more ideas
       I'm bent over backwards for elastic pleasure
& streamers & ribbons & thunder & technicolor lightning

& as I speak poetry the coffee shop dissolves into words
       that scribble a pair of boys' new white shoes on the floor
& a pale human body in the next poem starts to cross the street

(poem six – unfinished)

& the Downs Syndrome kid sets up in Oliver Plunkett Street
       scrapes the scribbles off the strings of his *violin* [del.] 'fiddle'
& a man laughs in tears pointing in fathomless cruelty…

René Van Valckenborch and Robert Sheppard

Jānis Raups (1967?-)   Latvia

From *The Refutation of Colour*

6

I am a dentist at the mouth of the Daugava
unconvinced by colour or the riparian
rippling of light in its chaotic
kaleidoscope. As colour blind as Scott Walker
torch-singing the incoming light to grey; I know he
slays the whiteness of the whale, to deny the glare of capital.
I know the pupil is an ocelus that fans before me,
a pellicle over a gulf of vigilant invisibility.
There are weeds under the tongue of the Daugava,
there are weeds in the absent beds of the Poliklinik at Heidelberg.
They share no hue.

7

I see him, Patient Walker, trapped pupil
on *Scott 3*, lashed
in the panoptical gash seeping mauves
the bruised moves of iatrocracy.

Its blink flared with orange bursts and
radiating white capillaries across broken blue,
this organ registers him in bristles, in prickles,
Engel, Engels. You maul a medical manifesto

in the hollows of the waiting rooms of the Doctors' classes;
skrike Saranwrap odes to madonna-grey days
on the cellophane streets. It's raining today
our saturated sight must wash colour away,

collachrymating the vanished distinctions.
Grey haunts the scene like a concept with which
no-one feels comfortable, muggy-dank under
Baltic thunder, shaky framework dumped over reality.

SIMON PERRIL AND ROBERT SHEPPARD

Jurgita Zujūtė (1966-)   Lithuania

Insomniac Division

the corridor greys out shades
its own shadows as eyes adjust to this invitation
in a crack of darkness

equally a threat this restless blur
bleaches the world

an orange claw twitches like a glove
and flexes toward you

if it points it points at you

*

droning into consciousness you blink off
each wave of vision

the floor resists its shaping
the wall crackles against a world of silence
a dream floats across the room a filigree
of narrative stitched by chance

cuticles curled like a curlew's beak

*

shadows envelop your lids

the white eyes flash your way
for one instant the night judges you finds you wanting

it
squats on your collapse the panic
not quite reaching the unlocked front door

*

the dotted line marks the kerb
follows the long curve of the lamp-lit bridge

to her blank-faced animal relief

the forest of surveillance dishes behind her
as her piss sparks on the wire fence

static streaks across the screens
of the state's night-shift vigilantes

*

purple leaves tumble through the night
from the sky-map of my conscience
constellations form from my desires
a flung string of pearls refuses to configure

against a black so shiny it's silver
scented with a sheen of ink

*

the brown ground is webbed with the roots of spectral plants
under subfusc trees that shelter us during the day
we build a man from limbs of light
and he walks towards us promising the world
scratching the eyes out of night's hood
spirals of light weave impossible places
skittering across the skies in meteor showers

something should give this
the chance of a ghost

*

she closes her eyes and reads

it rustles
and shuffles like bodies or feet and is
telling us something or trying to

heads burrow bite
into the dark heart of the city

this moment made it as plain
as this blacked out theatre of real things

weak pin-pricks glimmer
act out a kind of pathos
between phone booth and electricity box

cartoons of trace etched on slate

*

amid a mud paradise under a brown sky
I tempt a dream to take form

curling in the distance
stirring into stems that droop
as they rise

a splinter tears the sky

one searchlight its beam
marks the speckled forest floor and builds
half a shadow on its own shadow

its promise
bathes the open ground a mirror
full of cities on fire

ROBERT SHEPPARD

Georg Bleinstein (1965-2046)   Luxembourg

as a dullness, as a gaol

vow¡[woo Shelia   oaf UGu(of

      Book(ahoy á ñ ž c¬:A.

war you Oaf (one aqua   Had´

        moa.

TOM JENKS AND ROBERT SHEPPARD

Hubert Zuba (1964-2015)   Malta

AND OUT.

New arrival in port. Ditch the goods;
dump the van; drop the mood. Full-
throttled silence: find on these kinds
of tiller your misplaced misery.

Ship your broken affairs. Throttled
silence on a free rock. Is pay alert,
for nose hulls of worn swimwear and
drying sheets soiled with misplaced love,

exuding a sickly sexuality as though
they've been fucked by ghosts? If arranging
the aircraft kits is out, scooping these islands

together like beans in a stew, determined prime
to breakers, we'll slither down the storm drains,
slip away to our miserable Mother. The only way is down

Scott Thurston and Robert Sheppard

Maarten de Zoete (1963-)   Netherlands

Orphic Voices

On the Trans-Historical Railway
                    we could traffic you know
what with Cendrars or arm-wrestle
                    with Álvaro de Campos
iron bolts bent over backwards as in
                    a volume of Huidobro

Orpheus tornados the action
determined cranes
                                        scatter across the floor
into the less than nothing that could hide
                    apolitical Samson
who has too much to say

Next the tracks' infinite surveillance
                    circle road blocks the drone of more than I get
the word delivery amounts to no posturing
                    as vectors for victors
                              a book makes the poem
refutes the bomb-plants to leave open plans
                    to cluster bomb chemicals of poems
says the power

We transit in levity
                    and obligation

with a lament for gunfire popping to sink
limitless data-voices in this orphic rising

GOD'S RUDE WIRELESS AND ROBERT SHEPPARD

Jaroslav Biały (1962-)   Poland

Museum of Polish Military Defeat

From Wikipedia the free encyclopaedia

This article is about the Museum of Polish Military Defeat.
For other uses, see <u>Polish</u> (disambiguation)

In Głocwak, that which has disappeared is a defeat...

Artefacts:

rubble
rubblestone piece of broken glass compacted haikugrit and endmote a
dactilar printpart of shard perhaps someone threw

blood
someone's pump&pulse even and especially when they're least aware
of cells flowing in the same unriver that bluered liquiheat we think can
feel or is part of sentient us rosy thing that splatterdrips heraclitusly
veinfully b'doom b'doom b'doom b'doom d'boom until the pressurevalve
collapsydooms

rat

brick
the second law of thermodynamics states that the universe is moving
forward irreversibly and can't undo the baking of the brick so that the
brick is never unhardened back to the state it was in when we stepped
gingerly across the raindrunk field and never reverseeing the dynamics
of the heat and the done things between us

melted candlewax from a vanished church
someone's rainbowdoves nest down into reality as deaf easter disaster

stiffens in plaster now dragon dragoons are speared by harpy diagonals
we're beaten/bested/worsted sour enderers to the whollygoest holygon
waxenwaning stickywicked lost&peccative mission

missing button from military uniform
is the uniform present without the button? is the button present without
the uniform? in either case where is the military? what is the force of the
word 'from'? button this occasion the meddlesome thing depended on
a stitching wartime a miss needling

hipflask
mudthudglug the Waterloolooloo battlestop
thwarted the foiled nose of the pelagic wreck
pushed into the tankasand seabed
we're pissing a line of our elegy
to borscht
as crabhaired trembleful shudders

the container spills all mouth halfplug glug'
glug'glug'glug'
glug and no bottle stop

mud
if only it could be eaten
mudworm of unknown misadventure and even mud
is rationed
my organs fail
fail mud would poison the worm
I am less than half a mudmad man
pride of my failures
poa nobilis holding firm is all
chrysanthemum zawadzkii
to withstand the advance

rain
raintroopstroopstroopstroopstroops
rainshotsshotsshotsshotsshots
raintrenchedtrenchedtrenchedtrenched
rainp.o.w. p.o.w. p.o.w. p.o.w. p.o.w.

rain**faultfaultfault**
raincaughtcaughtcaughtcaught
raincowercowercowercower
this foreign reign unending reign filters through the drops
shots reign through the trench faltering reign
troops drenched in gangrain   everywhere
the enemy rains

id tag with no name

jaroslavjaroslavjaroslavjaroslav
b   ł
i   y
y   b
a   i
jaroslavjaroslavjaroslavjaroslav

rusted blade
rust&dustwound
          on the eye that draws down
glassvitrine   baize   fadedfabledfadedlabel
                    'rusted blade' or 'Lithuania. the ghetto'
the poem deprinted there

curvycrust breeding metal fatigue men in fatigues (once)
curvacuum of manspace mantime
advent(curvat)ure of archeopaedic spacetime
('curvaceous' (suspendered in wartime brothely-broth))
curvifoliate scratters
curvated curiosity cured on *huk!* impact
curviform steel ensanguined in hacked beguine of
curvity&hakenkreuz

tears
veiledphial

verified
          pistol clean

70

crystal lens

saline a line say a line
saline a line say a line again
saline a line say a line again and cloud
judgement with

misted vision
          (listed mission)

nameranknumber on the file

lachrymale bonding in the smudge

searchlight beams dispersing into thickening cloud
'spongelight squeezed dry glimmered smokerolls
collecting in the mirrored palms of night closing
into a dark prayer over a splutter a stutter of gunfire
the cloud falls fills the air we breathe across the misted land'

(the warpoem printed next to the artefact takes the breath away
takes the light&dark away &then takes the artefact awayaway)

Affects:

Indifference
who cares who scares whose cares – and beyond bzura, tarnów
                                                                  who should
what is blood   these hands   what is the shedding the herding
          through mIasto-mIasto-mIasto-mIasto

our midastral selves $^{divided}/_{defeated}$
our arms $^{un}/_{real}$ tied=dumped in pits   at the stride of the road

our $^{c}/_{limbs}$ dejected+subtracted

we knew contradiction spiralsmoking from the formulas for reality
system $^{t}/$error
$^{life}/_{death}$ foefriends fiends
and what of it when
                  distancedulls
                  disbelief
                  danzig corpsefields   and nothing adds up

Faith
Reversed time questions, passed states, past states, on the basis of known future states, probability of future states rather, cannot be time-symmetric, the second law issued/issues/will issue its warrant, in the future direction only, striding, where such excuses will not be needed, will not apply. Your third widow watching the scrapping of the fleet at Gdansk dry-dock. Frigate's skeleton floating on air. Anchor clawing a cloud of battle-smoke. Undrowning sailors marionetted by parabolic-silk sky. Sky silk-parabolic by marionetted sailors undrowning. Smoke-battle of cloud a clawing anchor. Air on floating skeleton frigates. Dock-dry Gdansk at fleet

Betrayal
A door disclosed
A whispered wor(l)d
A hiding
S.now
A bicycle leaning against a fall

Cowardice
spy
spy
retreat hold breath
spy
thrump*thrump* thrump*thrump*
dilation of pupil dilatant widedropped

oval as drip
of pppersppp pppersppp ppp

Fear

Self Immolation
'War Poem' by Jadzia Biała

'leaves in the park rustle
as children kick through them. I?

water fowl burn white
upon the dark water, and a great

squawking flap of desperation dives
into a pool of flung grain. I?

the heron waits alone, alert. I
circle its lake, driven, catch

a whiff of decay where
the water stagnates

in a leaf-choked corner, as I…
I? I? I?'

Pride

Ambivalence
outwitted outshone in defeat
in retreat the feet beat from a fleet-bleak peak
in surrender render ender

in occupation they mime German bazookas Russian mazurkas
in resistance (coded ode in the fixed abode)
in liberation dusty flagrag on the rusty pole-pole
in prosperity the blacksmithmillerwheelwrights of Troy de-sacked
in expansion our pierogi guts in the festive square
in militarization 'our' militarization
in conflict Kock corpse-copse blossoms once more
in warfare outplayed outwitted outshone
in defeat in retreat in surrender in

Regret

[   ]

ANAMARÍA CROWE SERRANO AND ROBERT SHEPPARD

Ana Cristina Pessao (1961-)   Portugal

Sixth Letter to Nympha Negra

Dear aunt Nympha,

Thinking of you is thinking of a fountain with white water lilies
touched by a shadow

    a young immortal goddess that springs out in the night to
perform Bacchic dances with Satyrs

    and yet I fear your dark hallway lined with mannequins of Italian
marquises, the pulleys that operate the contrivances for the séance, O!
aunt,

    dear aunt, I relate my longing to your writing; your poems reveal
to me that the same blood is flowing from generation to generation

    you stand with soaking parasol on the gangplank, arriving, your
little travelling bag stuffed with the secret charades you write for *him*,
with your translation of Brockden Brown (oh, the minor distinction
of one who inhabits the voice of another)

    looking at my young reflection under the veil, I see a bride I fear,
a whiteness touched by that same shadow,

    a waxen face hovering in the black mirror, my death mask
wedded to your life mask

    dank nuptial gowns steam musk like a dying mammal

    and I want to escape into the night, like you did

only you can understand this dullness—say

    where is my freedom if I cannot reach the arms I desire when I
desire them and what desire is this desire I pretend—say

aunt, under the brocaded lampshade hooding the light, your words' colour and vitality concentrated like poison, speak to me with your trembling hand—tell me

is the labyrinth of desire twisted in your mind like a map of your mind, as is mine?

yrs, anna

Nineteenth Letter to Nympha Negra

Dear aunt

I did it. and freedom had the taste of sap running through myriad branches of a rootless tree

aunt, loneliness is now its ripened fruit

I am here, nympholept of your clenched womb

The sky drops like a blanket over your bones. Now you've returned you can liken anything to anything. the tingle of a bell. A foot in a glove.

'blood oozes from crushed flesh like juice from an orange,' you quote *the* name that remains the same

I placed myself at the centre of that twisted map. then it began to crumble and now I have it wrapped around me the paper, tightening me with its streets and parks and streetlights and fountains and with its shops and markets and all the languages that dwell upon it
wrapped up like a plait
or a tower that grows from disquiet to return to the beginning
we keep returning to the beginning but it is A beginning
a familiar silence

that dries your tongue like a ripe persimmon
                    after which you cannot swallow
I did it. and all those charades you wrote for him turned my stomach
          into a great laughter
I've finished *Wieland*

          during the séance, you slump forward in a deadly nod, towards
futurity, me. I did it. Uncharted marine depth, unfathomable freedom.
You enter its jelly world. the pelagic nymphaeum of the undrowned

          Oceanic disruption! Octopi Personalities!

     I now know it was never a game of reflections but the same waxen
face hovering in the same black mirror

          as the Bairro Alto quickens, You adjust your bonnet, like the
          shadow of my doubt, tickled by flirting breeze, and cross the same
          road into my dead dummy arms, your nymphae atremble, a
          black beginning. you did it

Yours forever

Ana Cristina Pessao

JÈSSICA PUJOL I DURAN AND ROBERT SHEPPARD

Mirela Nemoianu (1960-)   Romania

From *Cave of Bones (Pestera cu Oase)*

for Herta Müller

Strofă 7

I.

space opens up inside us
not carrying flowers
not wearing a veil
it is different for each of us
space opens up
your mouth for his
sharpens my desire

II.

flowerless
without a home
it's difficult for both of us
we respect the rules
your gaze
shares my desolation

Strofă 15

I.

light casts a face into the mirror
or rather
her eyes looked like mine
one final word in my mouth
after hours of questioning

II.

       light-headed   misaffection
       or rather
             misdirection
       to anyone with eyes

III.

       my light-fingered lover
       stealer of hearts
       our love should be
       a notifiable disease

Strofă 29

poppies and lichen at the corner of the green
a heron hunched on the riverbank
lock gates pushing against the weight of water
let a trickle into the weedy depth

I cut up old books about space and insert spaces
into them every leaf-turn a conjuror's name-day

your face tilted over the piano keyboard
clawing your way up and down an octave

gloaming pathways where only memory serves

Strofă 41:

          night meets
          with blame
          night targets
          enemies
          schemers

bluenose night
in gaslight
in mines
stunned
distraction

Strofă 49: little tears

I.
offsets   such   inner
fur   jaded   wonders
offends   such   dim
fur   shaft   winch

II.
far   suns   bide
hire   unstruck   lichen
tilt   hired   writ
ash   wine   mars
letters   mines   mind

III.
niche   becomes   order
    jaded   forage   zoom
    stellar   unsure   libel
    soil   eyes   meld

Strofă 64

for Erik Satie:

now fierce winter
guards eyes pent-up

lichen

acute Dorinda

flowerless portal of esteem
deficit   abandoned
buckled   parted

my poor degraded

                    radical

                              orchid

one final word

                    means

                              disaffection

tendresse   behind bars

lubricated gangsters

            in the animal hotel

Strofă 75

I wanted to go to a place
that did not know who I was

I was wrapped in silence
so deep and so long that

I cannot unpack myself in words
when I speak

I'm just a little different package
I was my own thief

the words came nowhere and hit me
many people think to pack a suitcase

is something you learn by doing
like singing or praying

if you do not have the right things
improvise

turn right
            things needed only things
simply because they are what you have

novels because they are read
only once and never

Strofă 79: from my desktop

this single letter
        gives direction
where you'd like to be
where I do not know
        who I am

        plum brandy and a handkerchief
                            of clouds
those blue and yellow days
in coffee-shops and hotel-rooms

beneath the linden in Cofou Park

lost footsteps in the railway station

the black Mercedes with motorcycle outriders

Strofă 85

time closes down outside you
dust on the screen furs my body
as I climb in darkness onto a wall
projected against ironic icons
my frown in Iasi flustered turns
I smoke a cigarette between red lips
as if my last and the spouts of these boys
darken
my dark hair hangs loose like a thought

my heavy hearted enemy
flat against the wall in a silvery gown
packs the leu down her cleavage
the news is breaking the film cans
burst pipes vomit black radiator fluid
whatever happens
carp rest below the algae cooling
or become form growing sleek
are transformed

darkness sucks a body out of the shadows
the long years' booty a crop of images
breaching the blind cure of unknowing
arms outflung in an embrace of multitudes
tear gas tearing through our peaceful protest
a milky film peels away
like an ear coiling the siren calls itself
a naked account of undraped this
and stripped down that

dessicated policemen outside the mineral zoo
tense against the world secrets to themselves
extending across the earth's rim
between the spaces that create space
it moves motive
dissipates into multiplicities they cannot follow
a non-aggression pact at the heart
of Europe where they flush out partisans
from bricked up buildings
and march them off into family trauma

Strofă 100

(my new lover re-tuned the viola
our glasses of Muntenia red untouched
we inhabit the silence like stiff gloves
his fist rests on the table
in steely fortitude

if the waiter doesn't appear soon
something will snap
black-scarved widows hold mugshots
wrinkled flesh pages
for the pale and faint clientele

insufficient service with our aching tongues
haunts the frame of our honest loving

earish Monday's vendettas
sicken and die
                    hash-licked
plaits in the melt

ROBERT HAMPSON AND ROBERT SHEPPARD

Matúš Dobeš (1959-)   Slovakia

As I drank double espressos

As I drank double espressos in the shade outside
Shtoor, the parade of fashionable women with
their lapdogs and laptops lusted after my
chestnut cheesecake. Illuminated by headless
hats I swallowed a slice with powdered moustache
and wiped my mouth across my silver sleeve to
disgust them all. Still the Castle squatted over the city swelter
until lightning slashed its pronounced silhouette, keep of
The Golden Treasure of Košice and the art of art
lovers. Besieged by a jealous sky the city poured into byways;
I dripped into the *galleria* of socialist realism.
Every stroke of private feeling, equivocal smudges
around the eyes, every shade of public thought, a mouth
of explicit driblets, small hand signals. Pictures of
health and happiness, paintings with titles like
The Industrialization of Our Countryside oozed from
the walls so I escaped into the glittering sun-sheen,
glimmering grey square. Already at ease, the musicians
had attracted a crowd; I nudged myself a seat beside a garish
pair of puppets, no less garish than I in my motley,
clown of the quotidian disaster. A foul-mouthed Russian
lurched onto a stage of his own imagining,
a fake-haired American leered into his camera
capturing a morsel of disordered flesh for consumption,
or ransom, mutually assured deconstruction! I fled to
the exquisite English Tapestries in Primaciálny Palace
which had me in mind of Marlowe, poor Marlowe, invited to a
deadly feast in Dartford, his fate not will, and here the secret
of Hero and Leander had lain hidden in the Hall of Mirrors
until I disturbed it with my dank presence, like George
Chapman lending his hand to completing the tale,
interloper-interpreter. Just George, who heard
Homer's heroes sing in the *Batrachomyomachia*, another
penniless poet in the city seeking a patron, croaking

out his days. I glide off into Perspex fountains, sculptures celebrating black holes, in slow-time now the work I was to do is done, I weave ways out of these eternal prisons.

JOANNE ASHCROFT AND ROBERT SHEPPARD

A.B.C. Remič (1958-)   Slovenia

If I Were...

If I were a blade of grass
I'd be bending in the wind
like all the others, in the wind
off the Karst that smells of the sea.

If I were rowing in the ripples
I'd be unrolling in crinkles of
light against the hills, distance
unthreading perception, gently.

If I were empty of perception
I could abandon History and encounter
The World, my enemy, my friend,
my teacher, in all its variousness.

If then, beyond Time, flung across Space,
a jay caught in a gust, I'd know
Identity is a silhouette bird acting as scarecrow,
choking up a paroxysm of irony.

If the scarecrow smiles, if Sirens
call lonely men on container ships,
and ghosts walk the leagues of grass,
then storm clouds, tribal wanderings, ritual.

If overhead wires trapped onto a page of dashes
tell us of nothing, or next to nothing,
then the solid black I feel is not ghostly solid:
my ears are up to my eyes in Reality.

Slovenia (excerpt)

An advertising hoarding of a rearing horse,
a railway platform reduced to a grey smear.
Slovenia! I'm sick of your posturing, I'm weary
of your constant demands for attention, your angst,
even the tightness you leave in our collective lungs
that the romance of a steam-train cannot relieve;
the rearing horse is a symbol for a British bank,
the trains run on time, sure, but they take us nowhere.
Hills hunch black like slag-heaps, while streamed cctv
images of cobbled streets and marble kerbstones
infiltrate our dreams; a pixelated Ljubljana Old Town
lacking its charm and suppressed memories.
Lit buses in long lines ease up the crowded street
packed with faces at bright windows, and I run
to catch one, full of workers heading home. My people?
'hard-working, diligent and proud', the brochures say,
using my tainted words. A queue, stiff in readiness,
waits, as one, his pin prick pupils deep in their sockets,
like a bronze statue of one of our obscurer saints, leans
forward and hisses, 'You can't get on without a ticket.'

ALAN BAKER AND ROBERT SHEPPARD

Cristòfol Subira (1957-)   Spain

Freeze Block Station

(from the Spanish)

The cat sniffs the floorboards,
compulsive. The banana boxes
are full of dead books, sustained
immobilities. For resuscitation
I make my best impressions
of unshiftable listening. Hold,
until there are parrots in green
beyond the undrawn blinds. I
stand and read against the wall,
off kilter, overlaid with a pattern
of uneven shadow composed
by curtains knotted like fists.
Beneath the window, morning
unpacks a market of catholic curses.
Beyond, Montjuïc sings to the trees.
They listen for a rumba, tilting,
their upper limbs starched with light.
I stretch the skein of invisibility
over my face but I know that my brow,
nose and mouth push through; I
envy wrappers that no longer enfold
such dense befuddlements of stuff,
and find myself uneven, betrayed or
maybe freshened here and there,
by the slow baring of throat, or gut,
to the gutters of peripheral vision.
Eyes, nailed to a tree, animate
all these poses before the universal
disaster, a curtain call of small change
and foreign notes to be reworded
for bananas, peanuts from the kiosk,
biscuits for the cat who snuffles
in the small print for dropped coins.

Performance Between Two Points

(from the Catalan)

Balance
is a tenuous line to grip
with your toes.
      No hands. One leg.
      Closed eyes. Soft
moon landing of pointed
steps. A horse falls from a chair,
         a man melts
into a lamppost, a boat's prow-
ploughed zig
zag crosses the bay, while
        Falangist saints
lie petrified on low slabs and
     the Columbus Monument
twists its printed shadow around
      your middle
circumnavigating this navel
gazing delight as
you spin on a paving stone
     wrinkled for Gaudi,
and call yourself mime. Like
a bicycle
        stuck on the spot. But
        watch. Untethered, you
run in circles under the underpass,
trip into the alarmed mouth
     of your lover, drop
    by the café for a coffee and croissant
and dance your way through these mirrored
alphabets where,
    in the basement bar,
vowels blast open a black tobacco way
to haunt the Roman street below
    this street, or,
    from an attic flat,

a rolled R reels out to catch
the doves in flight and paint them
      pink
            with rampant tongues
of sunshine
      and even along the shady Carrer
D'En Gignàs you
wing, a rush of air, a gush
          of belonging:
as you prime trim space
with your becoming, twisting on a point
      moving along the paving, flailing
    your arms, settling
        on a spot, a dot
on the page, a stop fully stopped.

ALYS CONRAN AND ROBERT SHEPPARD

Kajsa Bergström (1956-)   Sweden

Two poems from *Flak* (Nonsense)

When one in pointlessness has come as far as I

When one has come as far as I in pointlessness
scraping the surface from the rock
each word enthrals
in a band that coils me and binds me to you
Finds in the loam
where I sink fast feet first –
which one appears with the archaeologist's shovel
mudman rising from the past?
The giant word I
buried within my tiny presence
perhaps a stone shard
hard that
some toothless man has used to scrape his morbid
wordmeat
The minute word you
scrubbed up in my astonished absence
maybe a pearl of glass
that once hung around another's neck
brought from the sunken grave-mound
keeps time from meaning anything at all

The silence of the yawning is vast

The silence of the yawning night is vast
unspittled
It is not concerned with the scrabbling of human beings
who, vastly overmouthed, devour each other upon the shoreline
crunching bones and gulping sad flesh, fluids…
And I can hear
though the ear is folded upon its own echoes like a shell

the glorious watersound
from ships who sail
upon the sea out there
with bleak parrotvoices of beaky fulfilment
the shanties of the sandy respite of the Pseudo-Crusoe
These ships, are they truly so naïve? so predictable
like little ferries crossing to the little islands...
Sometimes I hear from out there the drawn howls
of the living... of the dying...
as though... as though...

Trettiofyra

the expected time nears groups
louder than an art work past

the
shut nestling into our own lefts and then
undulate forever identities gathering near
the ink shop the sex shop underfoot
the road tramlines still
ghosted under people with
collective

the bar with
self-involved news she carries the people
of Malmö down the cobbled
surfaces

a taxi of self-identifying
from Copenhagen with tiles
its wallpaper its
cherry soft resistant
while the secret mountains
she harbours
beneath the one headlight

picks us up with
its fat legs

the shaved heads are scraped plaster
peeling

she does it the language
leaves mulch down at the corner
and we're gone with self-possessed ease
the
elderly vegetarian restaurant
is conventional as
on the pavement blankets

three men approach carrying chains
and couples (who
look as though
they've
witnessed a hive of health
revolt not now as
tearing she edges to kerbs
creates leads
for one moment
suspects the worst

it performs a slow
release the edges
of herbs to
create a
windows push
dusk gang
lost realising décor but she's not sure
where an illusion
we tip toe
that
dwarf

the body her thought is a gag on the overcast sky
is a shade between
across the play
we've just ceilings these dark warehouses

the men
of this final scramble
aboard tickets

her voice lost against the height
witnessed spills out t
he rules of travel
which have changed for high

S.J. FOWLER AND ROBERT SHEPPARD

Robert Sheppard (1955-)   United Kingdom

The Ern Malley Suite

> 'he was born in England at Liverpool'
> Ethel Malley

her hand grips her
letter
above the estuary

the slash of the horizon

sailing yawls
catch the breeze beneath
ecliptic clouds

his hand drips
blood
hoists a fetish

a pepper pot guffaw
snuffles
across flat waters

~

the elephant
stands four square
on the family sedan
levitating

full steam ahead

towards the warehouse
which is fed like a silo
but which fills
with levity

~

erect a statue in heaven as though
god needs another effigy
a Prometheus to lay eggs on his own plinth

as mere man back-flips above
the pools of England

to land on his feet like a real man
with doubly stolen fire in his prosthetic voice

~

her lantern-head and pinafore
announce her sullen
reappearance

on the path to the dunes

her Chinese wheels and chocolate box
ribbons steal the way to the dairy

his face moulded from mud
stirs to shake itself free

of dirt
but he brushes himself away

for good

~

jug too polished to grip
except to pinch the void
looped by its tiny handle

tilt it

full of cream
a thick ribbon
cascades into woodland

bucolic cadence
trills from a darkening branch tip

a malic mould singing

~

he's fallen behind the sofa
to find it alpine crag

crystal crests above sting his eyes
he hauls himself to his knees

to watch the grandfather clock
spelling out Swiss time

in stuttered Cantonese

~

plump stools complement the garish table
iron sea monsters forged menace his toes

and a toilet pedestal for his stools
centres the ornamented chamber

mythological capers plaster the ceiling
sinewy wrestling and grunting

welcome to a shit under golden eagles
like his granddad in the Philharmonic

~

if a placid king penguin
were to waddle here
nudging its egg between
its webs

hands hennaed with Hindu geometries
might punch through the glass domes
of geological clocks
to offer it

a continent of drift

~

clouds printed on his nape
his broad back rises as cloud

shoulders a volcanic island
erupting into fictive cartography

as fresh as the isle of Frisland
its cities of Ocibar and Godmec

his panama tilts into a sun disk
or twitters for a lark

Appendix
The Literature of Frisland, Ancient and Modern

The Tale of Queen Brenda and the Settling of Frisland

[The surviving fragments of the pergament most commonly known under this title were found in various states of decay and destruction. The Frislanders, like their cousins in Iceland, were a poor people for most of the Middle Ages and onwards and, being also provident and pragmatic, they would put their literature to the most sensible use they could – eating the hides or using them for clothing. The pieces reproduced here are not only the entirety of what survives of what was most certainly an epic poem, it is also the only piece of early Frislandic literature that has survived, excepting a few orphaned fragments here and there, none of which are thought to belong to this tale. Most of the poem was found sewn into shoes or bedclothes. Only the part describing the landing of Queen Brenda and her people (from 'Queen Brenda and her beserkers' to 'spotting the Island's first folk') was still kept as a regular manuscript, apparently read along with the Bible in evenings at a farm in Kapparún (Cabaru on the Latinate maps). All fragments, except for the one starting 'Song is but wind', which is a later discovery, were found by the Icelandic scholar and manuscript collector Árni Magnússon in the early eighteenth century. A wildly different version of the poem survived in oral form, through the Frislanders' rich tradition for singing.]

...circling the splinter of ice that centres the seas,
Creaking with prophecy: Eat no fish Frislanders...

... Queen Brenda and her Beserkers caught sight of bare land,
Where neither fox nor wolf,
      neither duck nor goose,
      neither tortoise nor turtle,
      neither rabbit nor hare,
      neither bee nor wasp,
      neither sheep nor an[t?]...

… raised to give praise: 'Oh Father that stenches like a Boar's spilt guts,
Oh Son who is scented like a Bear's aroused glands,
Oh Queen Brenda as fragrant as a Bride of the Briny Seas, we pour
Swine's milk cheese and bear's milk cheese as libation
Onto this magmatic shore that we name forever Frisland.
Joyful are boars when the swill is filled, and eager their eating.
Quarrelsome are bears as Beserkers when fearsome in the field,
Once dairymen approach. Swift are the eyes of Queen Brenda
Combing the steaming volcanoes and spotting the island's first folk….

… as a hammer crashing on iron to bolt a coracle, and thundering
Like thunder, he appeared. His body was smoked like a herring,
His spirit aflame like the rage of Hrothgar in a lost tale.
His mighty arms carried tongs in which he tossed molten metals
At the Beserkers. They hissed like snakes as they splashed in the sea.
Brenda sang unto the man:

> *Bjorn my best Beserker born of bears*
> *Feels no fear on Frisland's fishless shore;*
> *He bursts forth bearing crests of bear and boar*
> *And peels the flesh from living men leaving*
> *Sweetmeats and stinking guts hanging from gates,*
> *And widows' wombs torn free like bloody bladders,*
> *And children's brains bashed pretty hard…*

…'Song is but wind!' scoffed the foolish Frislandian,
'Music a fart through a sawn-off boar's tusk!'
'Insult not the boar or the bear!' she snarled, bearing teeth.
'I didn't say "bear". I don't know what a "bear" is. But I do know…

…Brenda the Perspicacious retorted,
'I'm trying to warn you Bjorn's not very nice…

… spearheads of spider venom mixed with…

... one or two thanes left living but crying forth for death,
Their napes uncapped and their brains pooled like dogs' vomit...

'... mark you, from Queen Brenda, the three causes of death: false
        desire,
Eating fish, and a lack of the thin stream of milk from pigs' udders.
The three sure sources of life are a boar's brawn, a bear's brain,
And the milk of ...'

... did speak Bjorn, still reeking with the gore of the last native
        Frislandian to resist...

    ... beyond the hefty hump of the volcano lay verdant vines...

                ... bloody bear-milking contests ...

        ... revenge for the misdeeds of hamingjusömu guð Boar...

...Brenda knew when she saw the faces severe of her twins newborn
That she had sewn division into Frisland's freshly fated fabric,
Deceived as she'd been by King Hjalti's double love manoeuvres.
        [interlinear gloss: 'see *Kama Sutra* page 39']
One son to the stony shore would retreat in resentment
As the other tended the vines in contented conceit.
Swooning into a dream (put there no doubt by God) Brenda saw
Frisland sinking into the Ocean of Despair, two men
Shapeshifted like Cuchulain, though into the guise of Boar and Bear,
And into each the other's slaughterer ...

Hróbjartur Ríkeyjarson af Dvala (1948-)

Koans of sweet pig Brenda and the escape from Frisland

1

The voice of fish
eating Frislanders.

The voice of terminality.

2
The sound of clapping
udders and titties.

Milk of the hound
or milk of the bitch.

3

Hissing snakes
in the country of adders
and udders
and nothing.

4

Neither fuck nor foe
neither lass nor lice
neither torpor nor corporeal
neither rabble nor whore.

5

This is a chest of food.
This is the Lebensraum.
This is the lock.
These are the legions of pork.

Mine is the breakout.

6

I'll give you salt for a bit of sea
or dowry for your biter-cunt;
the sound of one hand clapping
at my castration ecstatically.

7

Take this milk and drink it.
Take this milk and drink it.
Take this milk and drink it.

Drink it!

8

I fumble for your double love manoeuvres
in the dark

and scream the sounds of one eye dripping;
milk of the bitch
yolk of the hound.

EIRÍKUR ÖRN NORÐDAHL AND ROBERT SHEPPARD

Notes on Contributors

Jason Argleton was a student at Edge Hill University where his final dissertation was a comparative study of the poetry of Ern Malley and Bob McCorkle. He is pursuing practice-led graduate studies on Ossianism. Poems have appeared in various magazines, including *Pages*, and he translated Sophie Poppmeier's notorious *Book Two* into English. Argleton is co-curating an anthology of fictional poets, the United Nations Platform of Poetry (UNPOP) drawn from the approximately 200 nations (and disputed territories) of the world, from Afghanistan's Hamida Sulemankhel to Zimbabwe's Pakuramunhumashokoanowanda Nevermore.

Gurkan Arnavut's single volume of poetry is entitled *star/fish/city.* He lives in Cyprus where he works on Turkish language radio.

Joanne Ashcroft has poems published in *The Wolf* and *Litter*. Her first pamphlet was published by Knives Forks and Spoons press. She won the Poetry Wales Purple Moose Prize in 2013 and her pamphlet *Maps and Love Songs for Mina Loy* is published by Seren. She is currently a research student at Edge Hill University where she also teaches.

Alan Baker was born and raised in Newcastle-upon-Tyne, and now lives in Nottingham, where he runs Leafe Press. His collected poems were published by Skysill Press as *Variations on Painting a Room* in 2011, and his most recent collections are *all this air and matter* (Oystercatcher) and *Whether* (KFS). He has translated the poetry of Yves Bonnefoy and Abdellatif Laâbi.

Kajsa Bergström was born into a gentrified family in Ornskoldsvik. After brief periods studying in London and Uppsala, Bergström became a student of music in Paris and became familiar with the work of the Tel Quel group. Her first collection *Flak* (1977) was not received with any particular fanfare. She described its writing as suicidal. Transformed by her remarkable use of typography, her later work, *Songbook* (1996) and *Noli Me Tangere* (2005), written when she had moved to Malmø, balances her obtuse mysticism and her deeply personal intellectualism. From this time on, she began to accrue great acclaim.

Jaroslav Biały, perhaps best known as an artist, archivist and maker of installations (in particular his 'Museum' series), has been, under the influence of his wife, Jadzia Biała, increasingly committing his ideas to paper (or screen), though he has yet to publish a dedicated full length volume of this work. He is known world-wide as the principal authority on Leon Chwistek, Zonism and the demise of post-Zonism. Chwistek's influence on Biały can be seen in his early nonad compositions, which appeared as home-made pamphlets, where Biały challenges principles of formal logic, asserting the existence of nine levels of reality from which we interpret the world, including the abstract categories of invisireversibility and the incognifarious. Wisława Szymborska's seminal essay, 'The nomadic-nonadic of Jaroslav Biały' (*Literatura na Świecie,* nr 07-08, 1987, p. 416-421) was instrumental in bringing Biały's poetry to the attention of the literary world. To this day, Biały leads a nomadic life. In an interview with Jocelyn Goos broadcast on Polskie Radio Program II on November 13th 2003, he famously justified his lifestyle by saying, "Walls are unnecessary."

Georg Bleinstein was born in Grevenmucher, Luxembourg, in 1965, and by the age of six he'd published his first volume, based on the bilingual (German and Lëtzebuergesch) voices he claimed to hear in his head. Subsequently dropped from the Bleinstein canon, these hallucinogenic and hypnogogic poems, entitled *The Transitional Object Speaks of its Subject,* were greeted with derision and amazement in equal measures. (The title was provided by Bleinstein's father, the controversial TV psychotherapy guru, Georg snr.) The Hollywood actor Tom Cruise mentioned the poems in an interview with Oprah Winfrey in 1999, describing them as 'off the hook inspirational'. Cruise triggered unprecedented demand for Bleinstein's work in general and *The Transitional Object* in particular which the publishers, having long since been liquidated for financial irregularities, were sadly unable to satisfy. Plans to turn the poems into a film starring Cruise were reportedly shelved when the actor learned of Bleinstein's views on Scientology, which he memorably described as 'all salad, no sausage'. Bleinstein famously used this evocative phrase as the title of the hit song on the first (and only) album *Euro Autobahn Dance* recorded by his retro-Krautrock-cum-Ceilidh band, KraftCheese. A copy of this was sent into orbit in 2001 as part of the Luxembourg government's later abandoned space programme. Ironically, the name of the rocket was *Schenk,* in honour of Tatiana Schenk, a filmmaker, film producer and artist with whom Bleinstein lived in the early 1990s. Schenk and Bleinstein fell out over Bleinstein's claim for a writing credit for her 1995 film *The Sorrow of Canaries* and did not speak again.

Three volumes of verse, *Bleinstein's General Theory, Bleinstein's Specific Theory,* and *Bleinstein's Next Theory,* recycling familiar Luxembourgish tropes (eulogy to raw salmon, paradoxical encomium to poached hare, ode to black sausage and valediction to squirrel cheese) appeared in the 1980s. Bleinstein's poetry reached maturity in 1989 with the publication of *The Fall of the Whirling Ball,* which embraced experimental techniques learnt from membership of the Benelux Euroulipo group. His light-hearted use of their 'homophobic translation' constraint (an entire anthology of gay love poetry was 'translated' into straight argot) was disastrously misunderstood by the Luxembourgish LGBT community, who burnt effigies of him (memorably sporting a fleshly saveloy) during their annual Gay Pride March in 1990. Tatiana Schenk's support was vital to his rehabilitation and led to their short lived romance.

Bleinstein changed tack with *13,333 Ways of Looking at a Sausage*, a durational piece in which he wrote the same poem 13,333 times whilst looking at a sausage for 76 hours in an undisclosed location near Bochum. No footage exists and Bleinstein destroyed the poems at the end of the performance by plunging them into a deep fat fryer. The sausage itself is believed to have been purchased by Kenneth Goldsmith, who hailed *13,333 Ways of Looking at a Sausage* as a proto-conceptual masterpiece.

Expelled from the Euroulipo for 'conceptualist meanderings', Bleinstein fell into a deep depression and a cave while hiking in the Swabian Alps. He took up false flag pseudonyms to produce a multi-faceted poetic *oeuvre*. Even to this day it is not clear how many of the 1990s Submergist Poets were in fact Bleinstein in disguise, transgressing the Grand Duchy's motto: 'Mir wëlle bleiwe, war mir sin.' ('We want to remain what we are.') He is estimated to have been responsible for as much as 33% of Luxembourgish poetry published since 1995: from the works of Erwin Wertheim, Vampire Poet and schnitzel champion, to those of the minimalist enigma aurélian, author of *w*rst case scenario!*; from Jean Portante's innovative investigations of loss of memory and identity in *Le Travail du Poumon* (*The Work of the Lung*), to Claudio Lombardeli's nautical epic *Lushaborg* (the ancient Cornish name for Luxembourg), where the 'old sausage trick', as critic Titania Schenk put it, supposedly gave the game away. 'Wherever there's a sausage, present or absent, there shall ye find Bleinstein!' she declared. Bleinstein famously misquoted his father in his defence: 'Sometimes a sausage is just a sausage!' (Titania Schenk is not to be confused with her older sister Tatiana, of course.)

Even as late as 2014 when Anne Hoffman was commissioned by the Grand Duchy's Office to celebrate the successful sequencing of the salmon genome, Bleinstein was widely thought to have been responsible for her contribution, a 3D work of breathtaking complexity that used the sequence as a matrix for re-telling the popular Luxembourg children's story, *Sammy the Salmon*, in which the hero – catchphrase 'Oh Flip!' – navigates across land to Luxembourg by flipping to his spawning pond in Widow Martha's vineyard. When the piece was permanently installed at Place du Poisson Mobile in 2018 its flipping tail, farting gills and grunting mouth were a particular delight for children and adults alike. However, on one occasion Bleinstein was forced to publicly deny his involvement in a poet's work, when in 2001 Yann Lick was arrested for fraud in the Swedish artisan cheese market and further investigations led to accusations of his role in a poison sausage scandal in Ettelbruck (as well as plagiarism in all of his published works). Titania Schenk enthusiastically refuted Bleinstein's denials.

Bleinstein caused controversy in 2002 when he handed back his Theodor Blank medal, awarded for services to literature in 1998, in protest at the Luxembourg government's stance on commercial whaling. After this, he lived in Bitburg over the border in Germany, where, in 2007 a street was named after him. Bleinstein Straße has the added distinctions of housing the smallest branch of Kentucky Fried Chicken in northern Europe and accommodating no fewer than eighteen cheesemongers. In 2008 he narrowly missed being awarded Luxembourg's Batty Weber national prize. In 2011 he again missed out on the prize, which is awarded, every three years, for a lifetime's work, with many commentators blaming his intermittently colourful personal life for the slight, in particular his naming as a correspondent in the high profile divorce proceedings of Franco-German country and western singer and telecommunications heiress Aurélia Aulrich.

On 31 August 2012, Bleinstein made an infamously uncooperative appearance on the Luxembourg chatshow *Heiße Kartoffeln (Hot Potatoes)*, sporting impenetrable sun glasses, a heavy beard and a t-shirt bearing the slogan *Ich schoss JR*. Bleinstein began by stating that he had retired from poetry and would henceforth concentrate his energies on satirical ice sculpture. Bleinstein then proceeded to answer every question posed by host Ulli Ulrich with the word *Pute (turkey)*. It later emerged that Bleinstein had been paying tribute to English comedian, singer, actor and variety performer Max Bygraves, who had died earlier that day, referring to an episode of UK game show *Family Fortunes*, hosted by Bygraves, where a contestant gave that answer to every question. Bleinstein and Bygraves struck up an unlikely friendship after meeting on a narrow boat holiday in the Norfolk Broads in 1994, where Bleinstein was gathering primary source material for his uncompleted work of psychogeography *Five Mile Drain*. It is rumoured that it was Bygraves who introduced Bleinstein to the psyclobin mushroom.

Apparently serious about his retirement from poetry, Bleinstein spent Christmas 2014 in Greenland sculpting a likeness of President of the European Council Herman van Rompuy into the east face of the Kangerdlugssuaq Glacier. The sculpture itself took seven days. Bleinstein then spent a further fifty-six days melting it very slowly with a succession of matches, using some 40,000 in all. The experience cost Bleinstein three and a half toes lost to frostbite and he was badly mauled by a walrus. It also brought criticism from environmental groups and celebrities such as Dame Angelina Jolie, Dame Helen Mirren and Group Captain Carol Vorderman.

Perhaps discouraged by the Van Rompuy debacle, Bleinstein made a volte-face and returned to poetry in 2015 with *Snowflakes*, a series of haiku composed entirely of asterisks. In 2016, he published *Quantitative Easing*, a complex work combining macro-economics, micro-economics and macro-biotics, which Bleinstein claimed had cured his much documented bowel problems. In an interview in that year, Bleinstein stated that he had not eaten cooked food since sharing a tapas-style starter with former British poet laureate Andrew Motion at a dinner in 2011 to honour Nobel prize winner Tomas Tranströmer, after which he became violently ill. News of the damage to Professor Motion's trousers (and to his young female companion's stockings) made *Newsnight* in Britain, where it provoked Jeremy Paxman to issue one of his signature smirks and a *fatwa* against all poets. Bleinstein's presence at the dinner is mysterious given his much publicised dislike of Swedes. This is attributed by Bleinstein himself to being bitten by his father's vallhund in early childhood and reinforced by an incident where he became trapped inside an Ikea wardrobe he was assembling for his mother and had to be rescued by the fire brigade.

In 2018, in another appearance on *Heiße Kartoffeln*, by now hosted by former Italian pop star, glamour model and politician Sabrina Salerno, Bleinstein again found himself at the centre of controversy. Confused by the bright lights and struggling with hay fever, Bleinstein stumbled on his way to the stage and accidentally pulled down the trousers of President of the European Commission and former Luxembourg Prime Minister Jean-Claude Juncker, a fellow guest on a special live broadcast to celebrate the centenary of former West German Chancellor Helmut Schmidt. Juncker's underpants, a very brief blue affair emblazoned with the word *Butterberg* in gold, are credited with setting back the cause of European federalism some years. The episode made Bleinstein a hero of the Eurosceptic movement, with Nigel Farage quoted as saying that he would happily take Bleinstein to Sevenoaks for a sausage sandwich. Bleinstein replied gnomically that those who seek the sausage find only the chipolata. This remark proved to be eerily prescient when, during the UK general election campaign of 2020, Farage almost choked on a cocktail sausage in the green room of BBC Question Time, being saved only by the timely intervention of gardener and novelist Alan Titchmarsh, who performed the Heimlich manoeuvre with the assistance of London mayoral candidate Dale Winton. The ordeal caused Farage to retire immediately from public life and establish his globally renowned mail-order tropical fish business.

In 2019, Bleinstein again announced his retirement from poetry, this time to focus on ballet. His five hour long piece *Donaudampfschifffahrts-gesellschaftskapitän*, set, as the title suggests, on a Danube steam ship with Bleinstein himself playing the lead role, was premiered to equal parts acclaim and derision in Ulm in 2020. The production's run was cut short when Bleinstein, attempting an ambitious, non-choreographed vault over a mooring post, sustained a serious injury that incapacitated him for the next four years and rendered him incapable of riding his beloved racing bike for the rest of his life.

Bleinstein returned once more to poetry in 2024, when he narrowly won a bid against Anne Hoffman to compose a poem celebrating the Medium-Sized Hadron Collider built under Luxembourg City in 2021. It was entitled 'When Time Bent over Backwards', and was premised entirely upon the widely reported calculations of a Scottish scientist who had erroneously used Imperial measures instead of metric ones ('of whisky!' Hoffman sneered on *Heiße Kartoffeln*, as she infamously touched the bare thigh of Sabrina Salerno) to suggest that bright light was carried by dark light faster than the speed of light itself. When the sober re-calculations were released the funding body, the Schenk Foundation, demanded a re-write and Bleinstein produced a poem composed entirely of light in which, he claimed, as long as he bathed in its luminescence and he was visible, the poem was signifying. No wonder in 2026 he was shortlisted for the Batty Weber National Prize (though losing out to a scoffing Hoffman) but was awarded the prize at last in 2029.

Bleinstein became increasingly concerned with spiritual matters. In 2032, he joined the cult sect based around the life and works of renowned fishmonger and entrepreneur Harry Ramsden, spending six months in retreat in a restaurant in Guisely, West Yorkshire. The practices of the sect are shrouded in secrecy, with a number of former members being found dead in unexplained circumstances, often accompanied by a small pot of tartar sauce and a slice of lemon. Upon emerging from retreat, a morbidly obese Bleinstein was asked by a journalist what he had been doing and replied, in characteristically elliptical fashion, 'Battering a sausage'. The experience inspired his 2033 conceptualist masterpiece *Hake*, a transcription of the complete Harry Ramsden's menu on the reverse of a copy of the Maastricht Treaty. He followed this in 2035 with a companion piece *Haake*, a transcription of the complete Maastricht Treaty on the reverse of a Harry Ramsden's menu. Both documents were written using mushy peas and were completely illegible.

Now in his seventies, Bleinstein grew increasingly eccentric and was often accompanied on public appearances by General von Knyphausen, a tame puffin he adopted during a trip to the Orkneys. His later years were devoted to avian welfare and he ploughed his life savings into an ultimately disastrous owl sanctuary, whose collapse left him destitute. In *The Transitional Object Speaks of its Subject*, the six year old Bleinstein predicted the manner of his own demise in haiku form: 'dead at eighty-one / black bread in a wooded copse / the nuthatch attends'. This prophecy came true when, in 2046, a traffic officer found Bleinstein slumped beneath an elm in a picnic area near his native Grevenmucher, a solitary passerine perched upon his outstretched finger, pecking at the remains of a piece of pumpernickel. His reported, but possibly apocryphal, last words were: 'All things come to an end; except the sausage that has two ends.'

Bleinstein's translation of Dante's *Inferno* into asterisks, *A Snowball's Chance in Hell*, appeared posthumously in 2065. Its single sentence is uttered by a Usurer in Canto XIX: 'The one grace of being bald is that one / Can hear the snowflakes landing on one's head!' which caused consternation among the community of follicly-challenged Inuit loan sharks who had sought refuge in Luxembourg following the melting of the Arctic tundra. The work may be apocryphal (or the work of Hoffman) but was included in *Collected Poems and Doubtful Poems* which was published in 2086, coincidentally the year the first Luxembourger landed on Mars to establish Base Bleinstein. *All Salad No Sausage* was reprised as Luxembourg's interplanetary anthem, but the book was pulped at the request of General von Knyphausen, Bleinstein's literary executor, following pressure from the estate's Alaskan creditors.

Despite his colourful and eventful life, Bleinstein is perhaps still best known in the Anglophone world as Dirk Bloodaxe. Along with Blinky Peet, he is the doyen of Luxi Noir crime fiction, with his Heft quartet, featuring the portly and asthmatic detective of that name. The first of the series, *All Fat No Fun*, is about a serial killer who targets obese men, leaving at each crime scene an enigmatic KFC carton filled with lard and topped with a barely nibbled frankfurter. After an ill-fated trip to the gym, during which an exercise bike is pulverised, Heft realises that *he* is to be the sixth victim. (It was televised as a double bill by Channel 5 in 1998, starring Jeff Nuttall as Heft and Peter Capaldi as the villain, under the titles *A Fat Load of Good* and *The Plod Thickens*.) The novel's opening line set the sardonic and world-weary tone for the entire Luxi Noir genre: 'Heft had a way with women – it didn't work.' Heft's words have often been read as autobiographical, as Titania Schenk points out repeatedly in her study of Bleinstein's work and life, *All Gristle No Skin* (from which most of the facts in this account are drawn). (TJ and RS)

James Byrne's most recent book of poems is *Everything Broken Up Dances*, published in 2015 by Tupelo. He is Senior Lecturer in poetry at Edge Hill University.

Carte-Vitale is currently a resident of Paris.

Lucia Ciancaglini was at work on the epic poem *&* when she died in 2010. She lived in Cork and Pisa ('both towns with leaning towers', as she mysteriously put it), and previously had published three books of poems including *Pisa in Motion* and a documentary poem *Cork Gaol*, and an autobiography *Better a Death in the Family than a Pisan on your Doorstep*. At one time, she worked on the Channel Six soap opera *Vita e Morte*.

Alys Conran is from north Wales, and spent several years living in Edinburgh and Barcelona. She speaks fluent Catalan and Spanish as well as Welsh and English. She is the author of *Pigeon* (Parthian Books: 2016), the first novel to be published simultaneously in both English (original) and Welsh (translation). Her writing is found in numerous magazines including *Stand, The Manchester Review, and The New Welsh Review*. She is working on a second novel about the legacy of the Raj in contemporary British life. She is Lecturer in Creative Writing at Bangor University.

Paul Coppens' books include his masterpiece *The Fainting Goats of Moon Spot Farm*. His essay, 'Henri Lefebvre and Van Valckenborch's Poetics of Space' appears in Canderlinck and De Zoute's *The Transliterated Man*. He is the son of the film maker Paul Coppens, about whom René Van Valckenborch has written an essay, 'Frozen Cuts of Light: The Scratch Cinema of Paul Coppens', published in *Chosement* 1 (2010).

Kelvin Corcoran has published sixteen books of poetry and been anthologised in the U.K. and in America. His most recent book is *Facing West* (Shearsman, 2017). Shearsman has also published several other collections, such as *Backward Turning Sea* (2008), *Hotel Shadow* (2010) and *Sea Table* (2015). *For the Greek Spring*, a selection of his poetry about Greece was published in 2013. *The Writing Occurs as Song: A Kelvin Corcoran Reader* edited by Andy Brown was published in 2013.

Anamaría Crowe Serrano is an Irish poet and translator of Spanish and Italian to English. As well as having been anthologised and published widely in journals in Ireland and abroad, publications include *KALEIDOgraph*, written with Nina Karacosta (corrupt press, 2017), *ᵒⁿwords and ᵘᵖwords* (Shearsman, 2016), *one columbus leap* (corrupt press, 2011), *Femispheres* (Shearsman, 2008), and *Paso Doble* (Empirìa, 2006), written with Italian poet Annamaria Ferramosca.

Maarten De Zoete has published several books of poetry, including *Orphic Voices and Walk On Parts* (2015) and has a *Selected Poems* in preparation. In 2013 he made the TV documentary *Where is René Van Valckenborch?* for Danish Television. With Erik Canderlinck he is the editor of a critical volume on Van Valckenborch, *The Transliterated Man* (2014). Favourite band: Traveling Wilburys.

Ivaylo Dimitrov lives in Bergen, Norway.

Between periods of involuntary detention, **Matúš Dobeš** has published 49 books of poetry, many of them illustrated by his characteristic spindly ink drawings (for which he is best known in Slovakia). Inspiring a certain trepidation in the viewer, these drawings are symptomatic of deTrump Syndrome, a periodic and collective form of insanity characterised in its manic periods by auditory and visual hallucinations of rational absurdity, similar to those brought on by heavy and prolonged consumption of Diesel. A noted Anglophile, he has never visited England.

Sean Eogan now lives in his native Co. Sligo after moving back from New York. He is currently involved in a project of adaptations and 'translations' of poems by George Russell (AE) and Yeats.

Patricia Farrell's most recent publication is *A Space Completely Filled with Matter* (London: Veer Books, 2015).

Allen Fisher is a poet, painter and art historian, lives in Hereford. He is Emeritus Professor of Poetry & Art at Manchester Metropolitan University. He has over 150 single-author publications to his name. In 2016 he published *Imperfect Fit: Aesthetics, Facture & Perception* from the University of Alabama, the complete poetry of *Gravity as a consequence of shape* and a second edition of the collected *PLACE* books of poetry from Reality Street Editions, and a reprint of *Ideas of the culture dreamed of* was published by The Literary Pocket Book.

S. J. Fowler is a poet and artist. He works in the modernist and avant-garde traditions, across poetry, fiction, theatre, sonic art, visual art, installation and performance. He has published various collections of poetry and text, and been commissioned by Tate Modern, BBC Radio 3, and others. He has been translated into 21 languages and performed at venues across the world, from Mexico City to Erbil, Beijing to Tbilisi. He is the poetry editor of *3:am magazine*, Lecturer at Kingston University, teaches at Tate Modern and is the curator of the Enemies project.

God's Rude Wireless is an online cut up engine.

Robert Hampson's recent poetry publications include *Seaport* (Shearsman, 2008), *an explanation of colours* (Veer, 2010), and *sonnets 4 sophie* (pushtika, 2015). *Reworked Disasters* (Knives Forks and Spoons, 2013) was long-listed for the Forward Prize. He collaborated (with Robert Sheppard) on *Liverpool (hugs &) kisses* (2015). With Peter Barry he co-edited the pioneering collection of essays *The New British poetries: the scope of the possible* (Manchester University Press, 1993). He co-edited *Frank O'Hara Now* (Liverpool University Press, 2010) with Will Montgomery, and *Clasp: late modernist poetry in London in the 1970s* (Shearsman, 2016) with Ken Edwards. He is Emeritus Professor at Royal Holloway, University of London.

Hermes is the founder of Bongos for Rain, a charity which works with those in drought-stricken parts of the world to handcraft drums to invoke the Gods and provoke rainfall. Most of his poetry and word-songs circulate in handwritten fascicles or as sound files on Bandcamp, but his one print volume, *Working for the Healing Rain* is available from Lulu.com or the alternative bookshop on the edge of Zlatare. This volume was nominated for a To Hell in a Handcart Award in 2010. He was elected President of the EUOIA in 2016.

Jeff Hilson wrote *stretchers* (Reality Street 2006), *Bird bird* (Landfill 2009) and *In The Assarts* (Veer 2010). He also edited *The Reality Street Book of Sonnets* (Reality Street, 2008). Two new books, *Latanoprost Variations* and *Organ Music*, are nearly finished. He runs Xing the Line reading series in London and teaches Creative Writing at the University of Roehampton.

Eua Ionnou was born in Meligalas in the Peloponnese, a community she came to despise as a parochial tractor town redolent of manure and devoid of any thought beyond agriculture. Raised by illiterate shepherds, she ran away to Istanbul and made a precarious living as an unofficial tour guide and transgender magician. Whilst in Istanbul she became fluent in Turkish, French and English and, crucially, discovered the work of George Gemistus, Γεώργιος Γεμιστός the late Byzantine philosopher Plethon. Almost all her work, in the light of Plethon's teachings, is a single project – *The Golden Restoration of the Byzantine Empire*. This bought Ionnou into conflict with the Turkish authorities and led to her deportation. Her publisher Νέα Ορθόδοξη Εκδόσεις (New Orthodox Publications), closed down in 2008 two weeks after the publication of her magnum opus. The poem here is more recent.

Tom Jenks' books include *Sublunar* (Oystercatcher Press), *Items* (if p then q) and *The Tome of Commencement* (Stranger Press). He co-organises the Other Room reading series and edits the avant objects imprint zimZalla.

Minna Kärkkäinen is from the Käsivarsi area in northern Finland. In addition to *Choruses on Mars*, her debut volume, she completed a poetic exegesis of the Sumi language and, in the late 1990s, *The Need for Glaciers*, an extensive poetic treatment of climatic research. She has recently been engaged as a poet in residence with scientists on a classified Finnish research project, but this work is embargoed until 2055.

Trine Kragelund deposits work on a variety of platforms. Her work, or versions of it, exist equally as audio, film, video, either online as programmable/ interactive media or offline as site-specific installations with quadraphonic sound and hologram icons in occupied and vacated space, which have been exhibited around the globe, as well as framed on the page as codex-works. She eschews the words poet and poetry (and seldom appears in public or performs) and has won many literary and poetry awards. The work here, excerpted from her on-going non-linear textual intervention *NoNo*, was partly (un)originally sculpted from 'Google English', in her words. She lives in Christiania, Copenhagen, where she currently devises post-digital poly-media work and cohabits with the gipsy brewer Carl Schytte.

Frances Kruk is a Polish-Canadian poet and artist whose work has appeared in various international media. Her most recent publication is *lo-fi frags in-progress* (Veer Books: 2015).

Rupert Loydell is Senior Lecturer at Falmouth University, a poet and a painter. He has published many books of poems, the most recent of which is *Dear Mary* (Shearsman: 2017).

Steve McCaffery has been twice nominated for Canada's Governor General's Award and is twice recipient of the American Gertrude Stein Prize for Innovative Writing. He is the author of over 40 books and chapbooks of poetry and criticism. An ample selection can be savoured in the two volumes of *Seven Pages Missing* (Coach House Press) as well as in *Panopticon, Tatterdemalion* (Veer Books), *Alice in Plunderland* (Book Thug), *Revanches* (Xexoxial), and

Parsival (Roof). His book-object-concept *A Little Manual of Treason* was commissioned for the 2011 Sharjah Biennale in the United Arab Emirates. A founding member of the sound poetry ensemble Four Horsemen, Toronto Research Group, and the College of Canadian 'Pataphysics, he is now David Gray Professor of Poetry and Letters at the University at Buffalo.

Martina Marković eschews publicity, but she was born in Serbia and attended both the University of Belgrade, where she was expelled under mysterious circumstances (involving mushrooms that the authorities claimed were 'magic' and she pleaded were 'organic') and the University of Zagreb, where she studied history and politics.

Mirela Nemoianu was born in Ilsa and educated at Bucharest University, where she studied mathematics. After the fall of Ceaucescu, she joined Eurolipo, inspired by OULIPO and her dream of a borderless Europe. Her most recent work, *The Cave of Bones*, was written after the death of her long-term partner.

Eiríkur Örn Norðdahl is an Icelandic poet and novelist. For his novel *Illska* (Evil, 2012) he was awarded The Icelandic Literary Prize and The Book Merchant's Prize, as well as being nominated for the Nordic Council's Literary Award. In 2012 he was poet-in-residence at the Library of Water in Stykkishólmur, in 2013 he was chosen artist of the year in Ísafjörður and in 2014 he was writer-in-residence at Villa Martinson in Sweden. Since his debut in 2002 he has published six books of poems, most recently *Hnefi eða vitstola orð* (*Fist or words bereft of sense*, 2013) and two collections of essays. Eiríkur is active in sound and performance poetry, visual poetry, poetry film and various conceptual poetry projects. Eiríkur has translated over a dozen books into Icelandic, including a selection of Allen Ginsberg's poetry. He lives in Ísafjörður, Iceland, a rock in the middle of the ocean, and spends much of his time in Västerås, Sweden, a town by a lake.

Sandeep Parmar has two poetry books from Shearsman, *The Marble Orchard* and the Ledbury Forte Prize-winning *Eidolon*. She co-directs the University of Liverpool's Centre for New and International Writing and is Senior Lecturer in English Literature. She is the author of *Reading Mina Loy's Autobiographies*, scholarly editions of *The Collected Poems* of Hope Mirrlees and *Selected Poems* of Nancy Cunard. Her essays and reviews have appeared in the *Guardian*, the *TLS*, the *Financial Times*, *Poetry Review* and the *Los Angeles Review of Books*. She is a BBC Radio 3 New Generation Thinker.

Simon Perril's poetry publications include *Beneath* (Shearsman: 2015), *Archilochus on the Moon* (Shearsman: 2013), *Newton's Splinter* (Open House: 2012), *Nitrate* (Salt: 2010), *A Clutch of Odes* (Oystercatcher: 2009), and *Hearing is Itself Suddenly a Kind of Singing* (Salt: 2004). As a critic he has written widely, editing the books *The Salt Companion to John James*, and

Tending the Vortex: The Works of Brian Catling. He is Reader in Contemporary Poetic Practice at De Montfort University, Leicester.

Ana Cristina Pessao is a grand-niece of Nympha Negra who, when young, was a collaborator on *O Palrador*, 1902, and a forgotten author of charades. Pessao's 'Letters to Nympha Negra' shares the Gothic streak of her dead relative's work and is notable for a certain self-revelatory excess. 'This is dark writing with a layer of skin missing,' writes the leading Portuguese critic, João Pacheco, with some distaste.

Sophie Poppmeier's poetry includes *Book One* (2002), *Book Two* (2003), and *Book Four* (2015). She has lived in Vienna and Bratislava, but currently resides in Berlin. A neo-burlesque dancer, Poppmeier performed as Minnie Minerva (but occasionally – in Berlin – as Angela Merkin). Her best acts include the 'Ute Lemper Trilogy', based on *Punishing Kiss*, a 15 minute piece combining the swirling silk sea-waves and bejewelled seashell bodice-work of 'Little Water Song'; 'Streets of Berlin', a mimed drag-king boylesque; and 'You Were Meant for Me', in which she confronted the audience with 'unbridled displays of female desire', to quote a review of the time. Her later 'Narcotango' used the hypnotic grooves of Carlos Libedinsky's new tango for her exploration of intoxication, obsession and trance. In contrast, the energetic 'Neveen's Levee' involved Oriental and belly dancing. 'Madame Mallarmé's Fan Dance' was the most literary (and least appreciated) of her acts. Poems from her controversial sexually explicit *Book Two*, which abandoned the 'corsetry' of her characteristic four-line stanza, have been excluded from this anthology. Perhaps in reaction to the criticism of this book, she is said to have given up poetry and burlesque (on the brink of considerable success at the Berlin Burlesque Festival), but the truth may be less dramatic, since she studied Art History in Vienna, gaining a PhD in 2010. (JA)

Jitka Průchová wrote *Poems Ekphrastic and Plastic* while resident in Prague, where she worked in insurance. Since going freelance as a poet she has published five more books. She is currently writing a lengthy poem-biography of the artist Toyen (Marie Čermínová) of which the third instalment, *Artificialism*, was published in 2013 by Stěhovací Kabinet.

Jèssica Pujol i Duran is currently a Postdoctoral researcher at the University of Santiago de Chile. She was Poet in Residence at the University of Surrey in 2013/2014 and edits *Alba Londres* (albalondres.com). She has written and translated in Catalan, English and Spanish, and her poetry and translations have been published in various magazines and anthologies such as *The Dark Would: anthology of language art* and *Donzelles de l'any* 2000. She has two chapbooks in English, *Now Worry* (Department: 2012) and *Every Bit of Light* (Oystercatcher Press: 2012); a book in Catalan, *El país pintat* (El pont del petroli, 2015), and one in Spanish, *Entrar es tan difícil salir*, with translations by William Rowe (Veer Books, 2016).

Ratsky József is one of a small band of Hungarian organist-poets. Currently living in Brussels, where he curates monthly fusion events at the Maison Notre Dame du Chant d'Oiseau, Ratsky also teaches part-time at the Junfernregal, Brussels' school of Tonal Curiosities. He edits *Arrête!: The European Journal of Organ Stops* and lectures occasionally on metallurgy, particularly on the acoustic properties of antimony and tin. He has set his own poems, and those of Van Valckenborch, Atkins and Dimitrov, to music.

Jānis Raups is a poet-philosopher obsessed with chromatics, who has been sporadically working on *The Refutation of Colour*, a long lyric sequence in distrust of the neurological inconsistency of colour behaviours. His birthdate, 1967, is actually false; it is the date he learnt of, and briefly came into contact with, during time spent at Heidelberg University, Dr Wolfgang Huber, who went on to found the Socialist Patients' Collective / Patients' Front (SPK). Dr Arvīds Šneiders writes: 'Little detail is known about the extent of Raups' involvement with, or support for, the SPK. He certainly came across Huber in Heidelberg. But references to "weeds" and the "Poliklinik" in *The Refutation* testify to, at least, an acute awareness of the development of this curious organisation. It refers to a statement made by Prof Dr Hahn, on 9th November 1970, that SPK patients are like "weeds which can no longer be tolerated and must be weeded out by all available means". There is a possibility that Raups attended – as hundreds of participants from the Eastern bloc did – the annual meeting of The Working Congress of the Evangelical Academy in the Taunus Mountains in the North of Heidelberg in June 1971. Evangelism would not have attracted him, but the conference theme would have: "Self-Destruction: An Answer to Self-Destructive Living Conditions in Industrial Society". Reference to the "Doctors' Classes" is standard SPK pro-sickness rhetoric, advocating an authentic class struggle of patients versus the doctors who oppressively exploit sickness.'

ABC Remič was born in Lubljana in 1958 in what was then Yugoslavia. She studied Ancient History in Belgrade, then returned to Lubljana, where she still lives. Remič's experience of the fall of the Soviet Bloc and the conflict in the Balkans marked her poetry with a cynicism towards nationalism and authoritarianism, as well as a disenchantment with Western consumerism. She modelled herself on the American Beats in their opposition to war and authority, and translated Ginsberg's *Howl* into Slovenian. She has worked for many years as a copywriter for the Slovenian tourist industry, and her book length *Slovenia*, which has appeared in recent years in critically-acclaimed instalments, is due for publication soon.

118

Hróbjartur Ríkeyjarson af Dvala was born on Dvali, a small island (called Duilo on some maps) offshore of the larger island of Frisland in 1948. As a child he was deeply steeped in the folklore of Frisland, but after education at the University of Godmec in Historical Cartography, in 1976 he founded the Black Volcano Poets who abandoned the complex (and frankly inexplicable) metrics of traditional Frislandic verse in favour of open field metrics and post-surrealist content, with an American Beat tinge. An accomplished jazz vocalist, he spent a year at Berklee School of Jazz in 1978, but dropped out to concentrate on writing poetry and experimenting with hallucinogens. He taught at various universities in the US and, after a time as Visiting Writer at Argleton University in North West England, he returned to Frisland, just in time to become principal spokesman for the Ashen Revolution of 2002, which dragged Frisland into the twentieth century. Ríkeyjarson af Dvala was elected to parliament, the Lagadag, representing Ocibar, where he is a passionate advocate of Frisland's (apparently hopeless) candidacy for membership of the European Union. The poem here was composed just after he left Berklee.

Karla Schäfer does not exist. If she were to exist, Germany might too.

Robert Sheppard's first books were *Mutton-Shunters!* (Leg it: 1975), *There was no Quail-Pipe, though* (Raspberry: 1987), *Crinkum-crankum* (a rare foray into sound poetry after he attended Writers Forum workshops (he was subsequently barred for drunken behaviour)) (Tallywags: 1995), and *Tight as a Boiled Owl* (Bags of Mystery: 2000). Sheppard has since concentrated on longer projects, including a volume of acronymic versions of Tang Dynasty poems, *Come Home I'm Naked Already* (Spicket: 2008), *working the dumb oracle* (cracksman: 2013), *Exercising the Armadillo* (Sconce: 2014), and his magnum opus, *Cupid's Kettle-drums* (Taturtrap: 2015). His most recent collection is an autobiography, *Making Magic with Leftovers* (Waxed Giraffe: 2017). He lives in Liverpool with his partner, the opera singer Bertram Kaninchen, and their Rottweiler, Cecil. (PF)

Zoë Skoulding's recent publications include *The Museum of Disappearing Sounds* (Seren: 2013) and *Teint* (Hafan Books: 2016). She is Reader in Creative Writing at Bangor University and lives on Anglesey.

Damir Šodan is a Croatian poet, playwright, translator and editor, who graduated from Zagreb University with a BA in English Literature and History. He has published several collections of poetry and plays, as well as an anthology of contemporary Croatian 'neorealist' poetry, *Walk on the Other Side*. He has translated Carver, Cohen, Bukowski, Simic, O'Hara and many others into Croatian. Having worked for over twenty years as a translator for the United Nations, he is now a freelance writer and literary translator residing in the Hague, Netherlands and Split, Croatia.

Cristòfol Subira was born in 1957 in Barcelona. He worked for many years as a street performer and living statue in the tourist districts of the city. Between 1980 and 2007, Subira produced four collections of poetry, alternately in Catalan and Spanish, but since then, his poetry has not appeared in print except for several unattributed poems inscribed on the paving of cul-de-sacs in Barcelona, recently acknowledged as his work. There was one doubtful sighting in Brussels in the summer of 2010.

Philip Terry is currently Director of the Centre for Creative Writing at the University of Essex. Among his books are the lipogrammatic novel *The Book of Bachelors*, a translation of Raymond Queneau's last book of poems *Elementary Morality*, and the poetry volumes *Oulipoems* and *Shakespeare's Sonnets*. His novel *tapestry* was shortlisted for the 2013 Goldsmith's Prize. *Dante's Inferno*, which relocates Dante's action to present day Essex, was published in 2014, as well as a translation of Georges Perec's *I Remember*. A new volume of poetry, *Quennets*, was published by Carcanet in 2016. He is currently working on a version of *Gilgamesh* in Globish, the international business language.

Scott Thurston's most recent poetry books are *Figure Detached Figure Impermanent* (Oystercatcher, 2014) and *Poems for the Dance* (Aquifer, 2017) and a publication from Knives Forks & Spoons is due in 2018.

René Van Valckenborch is noted for writing in both Flemish and French. Publishing between the years 2000-10, his books (in French) include *masks & other masks* and *glance poems*. In Flemish his books include *The Fuck Me Shoes Chronicles* and the online *European Union Of Imaginary Authors: 27 Translations*. He was President of the EUOIA until 2010. A generous selection of his work, translated by Annemie Dupuis and Martin Krol, was published as *A Translated Man* (Shearsman, 2013), with an introduction by Erik Canderlinck and an authorial imprimatur from Robert Sheppard.

Hubert Zuba died in 2015.

Jurgita Zujūtė was born in Kybartai but now lives in Vilinus, Lithuania. Her books of poetry include *Night Songs, I Pissed on the Statue of Frank Zappa,* and *Nocturnes and Aubades*. She is in private practice as a psychiatrist. Other works include an academic study of stress among university professors, an account of the Rwandan genocide and a travel book about Greenland.

Lightning Source UK Ltd.
Milton Keynes UK
UKOW04f0854271017

311721UK00001B/63/P